BEYOND THE MODERN MIND

BEYOND THE
MODERN MIND

The Spiritual and Ethical Challenge of the Environmental Crisis

DOUGLAS C. BOWMAN

NEW YORK   THE PILGRIM PRESS

Biblical quotations, unless otherwise noted, are from the Revised Standard Version of the Bible, copyright 1946, 1952, © 1971, 1973 by the Division of Christian Education of the National Council of the Churches of Christ in the U.S.A., and are used by permission.

Design by Publishers' WorkGroup.

Library of Congress Cataloging-in-Publication Data

Bowman, Douglas C.
    Beyond the modern mind : the spiritual and ethical challenge of
the environmental crisis / Douglas C. Bowman.
        p.   cm.
    Includes bibliographical references.
    ISBN 0-8298-0847-7
    1. Human ecology—Religious aspects—Christianity.   2. Human
ecology—Moral and ethical aspects.   I. Title.
BT695.5.B695   1990
241'.691—dc20   90-31914
                                                          CIP

The Pilgrim Press, 475 Riverside Drive, New York, NY 10115

To This Fragile Globe We Call Earth,
and She Knows Why

The earth remains our mother as God remains our father,
and only the one who remains true to the mother
will be placed by her in the arms of the father.

—Dietrich Bonhoeffer

CONTENTS

PREFACE

in Countries of the G-7 World
We Have-more, who have turned this earth into a
Market Place

(We "moderns") are destroying the earth. We are wasting nature,
and everything we touch is becoming poison. The technological
and industrial engines that drive and enrich our living threaten the
existence of all life on earth. These facts no longer need to be
argued. They face us daily.

What is wrong with us? As some have said, the human species
is like a cancer let loose upon the biosphere and, like all cancers,
will kill itself by killing its environment. That is true, and if we
take time to look about us for someone "in charge," for someone
to blame, for someone to reverse this terrible trend, all we find is
ourselves and our huge, impersonal engines of technological industry that drive themselves and us to further destruction. There
is no leader to be blamed and no leader to be followed. Because all
are to blame and all are in charge, none are. Deep down we know
this. We feel helpless before the toxic forces that impoverish the
planet and the human spirit, and we tend to avoid the clear
message facing us all: Because of our inordinate destructiveness,
time is running out for the earth. Herein we may perceive the
fundamental pathology all our institutions currently suffer. All of
them—governmental, social, religious—tend to avoid the urgency
of the environmental crisis. That crisis is the primary issue facing
the world and should be fundamental to every agenda, but it is
not. We push the awful prospect of environmental catastrophe to
the back of our minds and get on with other tasks and other

thoughts. Feeling helpless and overwhelmed, we distract ourselves and drift toward that very catastrophe.

This need not be. We need not remain helpless before the progressive blotting of the landscape. I am convinced the human species can take a new evolutionary step. We can make a new beginning, because the way we think about and imagine ourselves and our world governs how we live. If we think of the world as an impersonal resource—there for the taking—we will continue to live like ingrates and exploit the biosphere like parasites. If we view the earth as a gift, a fragile child of God, a nurturing fellow creature, a new "Christ" wounded by humans and bleeding on a cross, we will discover a new reverence, and our lives will reflect that altered habit of mind and spirit. New images and new thought can change the course of history because they can change us, our view of the earth, and our manner of life as we relate to nature.

In this book I examine the issue of our thinking and our imagination where, I believe, lurks the real responsibility for both the environmental crisis and our complacency. I hope to open the mind and imagination to new possibilities. In doing so, I use two words in a special way. The word *modern* is used to denote the way of thinking and its attendant images that have dominated the Western world since the seventeenth century. *Postmodern* is used to denote a new view of reality that can move us beyond our present limitations by expanding our modern intellectual and imaginative horizons in ways that will enable us to live upon this earth without destroying it.

This postmodern way of thinking calls for radical and difficult adjustments in living, most especially in the wealthy nations of the world. It calls for radically new orientations toward family, wealth, property, technology, industry, economics, politics and the nation-state, war, agriculture, education, and religion. Every facet of culture will be changed. Every facet of culture must be changed. But accomplishing these changes depends upon a deeper internal change within each person—a change in thinking, a change in the imagination, a change in understanding the relationship between ourselves and nature. The change will not mean a new ideology that will contend with existing ideologies. The change is deeper than ideology. It is a change at the root of perception itself, one that will constitute an evolutionary transformation in humans that is as monumental as evolutionary advances of the distant past. It may be likened to the invention of a "new wheel," an internal wheel of the mind, imagination, heart, and spirit.

New thinking, new images, new metaphors, new spirituality, new ways of understanding the Scriptures, new views of nature, and new life-styles are already available to us and are being adopted by many. There is hope. We are not helpless. There are solid reasons for hoping in a future for us, for our children, and for the earth. In Jesus' own terms, there is hope that the reign of God is at hand now as before, and, in terms of the prayer he taught us, that the reign of heaven is possible "on earth as it is in heaven."[1]

The format I have chosen is simple. In Chapter 1, I explore the character of modern thinking and address the question, What is wrong with modern thought? In many ways this exploration is not a pleasant task, but it must be done. We must acknowledge and understand where we are before we can move on. We must feel and understand fully the chill that pervades our times if we are to move through that chill into the dawning of a new day for the earth. Here I also will discuss the images we use that reflect this modern way of thought—images of ourselves, God, the earth, and its creatures. We will discover how limiting, fearful, and destructive these images can be.

Relating thought to imagination, that is, to images and pictures, is important, because the particular images of reality we choose to employ can mitigate prospects for new thought or they can mediate new thought. For example, Michio Kaku and Jennifer Trainer have pointed out that the greatest innovators in modern physics often have been those like Albert Einstein and Stephen Hawking who have been able to see the overall picture of reality in new ways—that is, according to new images.[2] For them, the pictures or images come first, and "the math comes later." On the other hand, those who have resisted such thinking most often have been those who suffer from a mechanistic process of thinking, which means that they see reality as being a machine with parts that can be investigated separately without the need to step back and perceive the holistic, or overall, picture. We will see how this "reductionistic mechanism" governs most modern thinking and how it limits prospects for new thought.

Chapter 2 examines prospects for changing or expanding our view with the aid of what is called the "new" biology and physics, and with the rediscovery of what has been called the "creation-centered" Christian tradition. The new way, then, becomes a blend of what is very old and very new. This new way I also call a "vision," for it represents a way of thinking that expands to include the heart and the imagination. Thus, it requires the interplay of the heart and imagination along with the intellect. The chapter attempts to give the vision tentative articulation. Though it is tentative, I take comfort in the fact that visions require poetry, art, and song for their best expression. If caught and appreciated (and that is the point!), the vision will likely find its needed poets and artists who can help us translate its wonder into deep habits of mind and action.

Chapter 3 demonstrates for Christians how what is now called "spirituality" can take the lead in helping us adopt the new way. This is because spirituality involves primarily the heart and imagination and provides rich data for the intellect to ponder in the manner of deep spiritual experience. In short, I argue that spirituality will enable us to catch the vision of the new way. But the spirituality that can do this is new to us, even though it is drawn from Christian resources. I include a modest typology of spiritualities in the Western tradition in order to make vivid and to set off this new form from the dominant types in our tradition.

Chapter 4 relates modern and postmodern thinking and imagination to Christian life-style and ethics. In this practical and concrete discussion, I provide an example and guidelines that illustrate ethical decision making, action, and living according to the new vision.

The last chapter is a series of meditations whose aim is to bring the discussion to its conclusion in a manner that will challenge our faith, elicit new perspectives, deepen our ecumenical outlook, and transform our old ways of thinking about Jesus and his teachings.

But, like all endings, the conclusion makes for a new beginning. If we have the courage to follow its leads, that new beginning can change us—and the future of the earth and its inhabitants. Thus, what will be most difficult is the translation of what is on the following pages into our flesh-and-blood existence. We will need faith, courage, and tremendous inventiveness for that task. The promise before us is an advance for humanity and blessings for the earth. I think that such a task-filled promise has always been the substance of Christian mission.

As should be obvious, my approach reflects a Christian perspective throughout and is addressed to the ecumenical community of faith. It is my intention to set you loose for new forms of Christian thinking and living appropriate for this time of environmental crisis.

My thanks must be extended to David Ray Griffin at the School of Theology, Claremont, California. His January 1987 address on the character of modern thinking, given at the Santa Barbara Conference on a Postmodern World, provided the substantive base for my commentary in Chapter 1.

I must also thank Rebecca A. Rio-Jelliffe, Allen R. Killpatrick, William E. McDonald, Alton Robertson, Edward Williams, and Brent Waters, from the faculty and staff of the University of Redlands, as well as Jane Heald, of Support Source, and theologian-friend Laurence P. Byers. They have set straight my thinking with criticisms and suggestions that have improved my initial drafts and my initial thinking. Would that my book equaled their collective wisdom!

The editors of Pacific Theological Review were kind in granting me permission to weave portions of my article, "Toward a Post-modern Ethic" (Pacific Theological Review 20, no. 3 [Spring 1987]: 39–44) into the text of chapters 1, 2, and 3 of this volume. I am especially grateful to Stephanie Egnotovich, editor of Pilgrim Press, for perceiving a book in the manuscript sent her and for skillfully and graciously moving the manuscript from project status to book form.

Above all, I must thank my wife, Nora. She taught me the

mystery of the computer such that I could think and write without frustration, and she supported, loved, and tolerated a husband whose bumper sticker should read "I'd Rather Be Thinking." I am blessed.

BEYOND THE MODERN MIND

INTRODUCTION

Albert Einstein has written: "The unleashed power of the atom has changed everything except our way of thinking. Thus we are drifting toward a catastrophe beyond comparison. We shall require a substantially new manner of thinking if humankind is to survive."[1] His point was prophetic. Whereas we think atomic weapons may be produced for the protection of the nation-state, given their inordinate destructive power, atomic weapons make the notion of the nation-state obsolete. Ultimately they make conflict among nations obsolete. They make the earth an endangered species in the universe. Everything has changed *except our way of thinking*.

Einstein was not alone in calling for a "new way of thinking," nor is the issue of atomic weapons the only one that calls for new habits of mind. Theologians Benjamin Reist and Joseph Sittler have contended that the environmental problem cannot be addressed on ethical bases alone, because the dimensions of the problem call for new conceptualizations that transcend the ethical horizons of modern thinking, present a new view of reality, and lay foundations for a new ethic.[2] "We should do thus and so!" will not help. Present ethics, morals, and values are irrelevant, because the impending catastrophe is far too complex and global in its scale to begin to fit into the neat framework of moral rules or ethical systems of current thought. The crisis is the annual loss of billions of tons of topsoil. It is the overpowering of nature by billions of people—more than nature can support. (At current rates, the world in the year 2000 will be feeding billions more hungry mouths while 40 percent of the useable farmland will have been washed away, polluted, turned into desert, or cemented over.[3]) It is the weakening of the ozone layer of the atmosphere to the point of allowing death-dealing radiation to stream into our environment upon flesh that will react with the ravages of cancer, and upon life forms that will die of ultraviolet radiation from the sun.[4] It is the steady destruction of a chain of life that extends from the microscopic organisms of the sea to our own blood. The crisis lies in our life-style that has become so entrenched in protecting itself from the threats of nature, the threats of other humans and nations, and the threats of discomfort and poverty that unspeakably deadly arms have been invented in the name of defense against anything that would alter what we now are. Ironically, given what is happening, what we now are will vanish from the sweep of time in but a cosmic instant, a dream that was once called "humankind" but is no more. It will happen in twenty, thirty, fifty years—a twinkling of an eye in cosmic time. What current ethical system can begin to change any of this or reverse the inexorable trend? Reist and Sittler honestly acknowledge that no system exists for change. Our present systems are wasted, impotent.

What is important to note is that Reist and Sittler, who are not given to pessimism, have shifted the emphasis from ethics to what they call "conceptualization." They have chosen this word to refer to what others designate with the word *worldview* (from the German *Weltanschauung*, meaning "philosophy of life," "world outlook," "ideology," or "creed"). More recently the word *paradigm* has indicated the metaphysical and methodological presuppositions that guide scientific and other forms of intellectual inquiry.[5] Some, like Einstein, simply use the word *thought*.[6] Religious historian Ninian Smart points out that the English language does not have a single word that adequately designates the "beliefs and symbols which form the deep part of the structure of human consciousness and society."[7]

Conceptualization, worldview, thought, paradigm—each attempts to point to the substratum of human thinking that governs our orientation to our world. Accordingly, we may conclude that what Einstein, Reist, and Sittler[8] are saying is that the underlying presuppositions, structures, beliefs, symbols, and images of modern thinking are unable to provide the resources necessary for coping with the environmental crisis. Because these deep habits of mind produce the moral systems of the modern world, the moral systems themselves are inadequate. Policies driven by these systems in government, industry, agriculture, and religion are also irrelevant, and tinkering with them will not suffice. The axe must be laid to the root of thought itself, and a new way of thinking must emerge if the human species is to cope. In short, our habits of mind must change and expand from the bottom up. As we shall see, these new habits of mind will be attended by new images of the nature of reality.

So we must ask, What is this way of thinking that is called "modern"? What has gone wrong with the root of modern thought? How and why does it fail to provide resource for constructive policy? How and why does it set us on destructive paths? Then, above all, we must move on to the consideration of alternatives and the prospect of our adopting a new worldview, a new manner of thinking.

Part I

TOWARD A NEW WORLDVIEW

1

THE STRUCTURE AND LIMITATIONS
OF MODERN THOUGHT:
A THEOLOGICAL ASSESSMENT

Historians debate the origins of what is called "modern thought."
Many argue that it can be traced back to the seventeenth-century
philosopher René Descartes, the "father of modern philosophy."[1]
Others push the origins back to Augustine in the fifth century.[2]
Regardless of the origins, most agree that the essential components
of modern thinking are *dualism, mechanism, reductionism, materialism, determinism, individualism, anthropocentrism,* and *patriarchalism.*
I will discuss each of these in detail so that we can understand
them in theological and ethical perspective.

Before doing so, however, it may be said generally that these
isms produce both in us and in our outlook upon the world a
consistent and all-pervasive splitting apart of our perceived reality.
They are the ingredients of what could be called a "principle of
separation" that is operating in Western consciousness. Matthew
Fox refers to these ingredients and the fracturing they create with
the familiar image of Humpty Dumpty fallen and broken into a
million pieces.[3] This image is meaningful when we realize that
governmental, industrial, economic, and religious policies cannot
put back together what has been broken in human consciousness
itself. The policies are themselves the by-products of the broken
consciousness. They reflect it, and, with the breaking up of our
outlook upon the world, we break and rend asunder the biosphere,
which becomes itself Humpty Dumpty fallen.

Dualism
Dualism means simply that we view our world in a twofold
manner. We think our way into distinctions, not relationships. We

7

split the world into good-bad, right-wrong, true-false, successful-unsuccessful, friend-foe, mind-matter, mind-body, sacred-secular. Always dividing by two, we think we have arrived at a measure of understanding when we can say, "It is *this*, and not *that*." Everything must be set off from its opposite number to be understood in a useful manner.

Theological notions of dualism have existed for centuries. Dualism may take the form of viewing the world as governed by two fundamental forces—God (good) and Satan (evil). Augustine distinguished between the City of God and the City of Man.[4] Theologians after him wrote of a realm of grace and a realm of nature or of a spiritual and a natural existence. Dualism may mean, as Dietrich Bonhoeffer observed, "thinking in terms of two spheres," one sphere being sacred and spiritual, the other secular and profane.[5]

In Christianity, the dualism of the Western mind has always had difficulty, therefore, with the ancient, fourth-century Nicene creedal confession that Jesus Christ is both God and man, the God-man. John A. T. Robinson, twentieth-century Anglican bishop and theologian, acknowledged that for most this is an attempt to mix oil and water, and that one or the other ingredient is certain to drift to the top and be emphasized to the practical exclusion of the other.[6] The history of Christian thought and popular piety is replete with examples of emphases in both directions predominating at different stages. During the modern period the tendency among liberal Christians has been to emphasize Jesus' humanity—the moral teacher, religious genius, or prophet—whereas conservative Christians have emphasized the divine Christ, a superhuman equipped with supernatural power. Comprehending what the fourth-century thinkers attempted in forming a creed that said the unthinkable—that God was revealed in a man—strains our dualistic temperament to the limit. For us, the human and the divine just do not mix. What is finite cannot contain what is infinite. We have distinguished the natural from the supernatural such that a possible relationship between them escapes us.

Thus, Jesus Christ has become a mysterious reality we cannot fathom. He has become a reality removed from normal humans.

We do not seriously imagine becoming like him, really following his example, experiencing his closeness to God, and acting accordingly in our daily affairs. With that the movement he began is blunted and transformed into an institution that administers or proclaims supernatural salvation beyond this life. His dream of a reign of God "on earth as it is in heaven" is put away, denied, and not sought after. We remain locked into a 'practical secularism' in our daily affairs, and his great call to life with God on earth is scaled down and domesticated into religious institutions or otherwise put away as irrelevant to practical affairs. We cannot see Jesus because he is masked behind a split image of reality, that is, the natural and supernatural. Thus, we cannot think in the way he thought about reality. In the final analysis, he and his message become irrelevant.

The Nicene and Chalcedonian Creeds about Jesus were constructed on the basis of a dualistic image of reality that was popular in intellectual circles of the fourth and fifth centuries. This image, however, was not shared by many authors of the Scriptures, and certainly not by Jesus and his immediate followers. The authors of the creeds imagined a supernatural substance as over against a natural substance. Thus, if God (the supernatural substance) was in the man Jesus (the natural substance), then Jesus must have been a strange, improbable blend of this hypothetical supernatural and natural substance. Impossible? Well, at best, a "mystery"! One thing seems certain: Jesus is not like us, nor can we ever become like him. And yet, an assumption I will make throughout this volume is that it was Jesus' intention that we become as open to God and as God filled as was he, as full of eternal life as was he, as potent in the transformation of human life as was he, and, above all, able to think and love as he thought and loved. Such an assumption challenges the dualistic foundation of the creed and rests upon a new reading of the New Testament found in recent scholarship.[7]

Naturalism versus Spirituality

Another manifestation of dualistic thinking has governed the Christian view of spiritual life. In the West, Neoplatonic and

Gnostic modes of thinking of the second through the fourth centuries influenced Christian theologians, mystics, and scholars. The dualistic views of these philosophies created a tendency among Christians to deprecate the "natural" side of the dualistic equation in favor of the "spiritual" side. Things spiritual were viewed as good and worthy of attainment. Things natural were considered suspect at best, if not downright evil. This thinking led inevitably to asceticism, the denial of the flesh, as characteristic of Christian "spiritual existence." Everything concerning our natural, corporeal functions and tendencies was to be held suspect. Dualism, then, not only divides our world, but, in religious terms, it deprecates and denies one half of the equation. (I discuss later how this introduces into the West a view of spiritual life that is incommensurate with the outlook on life we find in the Jewish and Christian Scriptures.)

The images that attend this way of thinking about spiritual life abound in Christian consciousness, literature, art, and teaching. For example, do we ever view holiness as being other than elegant, effete, and delicate? What images come to mind when we utter the words *spiritual* or *saint?* Do we not follow the trend, common among Christians for centuries, of denaturalizing and dehumanizing the spiritual elite? Where does this tendency leave most of us concerning our images of ourselves? We see ourselves as all too human, natural, and given to questionable inclinations, from eating to sex! We would like to be otherwise, but being "spiritual," "holy," "saintly," is beyond us. This strange dualism creates two classes of Christians: (1) the very unnatural spiritual elite and (2) the semispiritual but mostly natural common person.

Dualism, then, as a root of our way of thinking, begins the subtle process of splitting apart the holistic connectedness of perceived reality into opposite, simple, static units or seemingly independent entities. We can master our world once it is cut up into distinct and manageable units, but the holistic richness of reality is lost to view. We cannot see the deep relationship among all things, and with that the whole of reality is diminished and distorted in our perception and appreciation. Once having distinguished things in dualistic fashion, we end the matter and do not press on to the next step of inquiry and question the relationship between the two elements distinguished.

I can best explain this by emphasizing the distinction between what I call modern and postmodern thinking. Understand that the distinction is made for instructional purposes alone. I do not intend to suggest a radical disjuncture between the two worldviews, but, rather, a development or expansion. The postmodern worldview challenges our confinement within the modern worldview, to be sure, but it does not deny the value of the modern way of thinking. It calls for expanding and developing modern thinking. Thus, we must appreciate the implicit interaction between the two ways of thinking as well as the tension created between them by the postmodern call to the expansion of our horizons. For Christians, the distortions produced range from our images of God and Jesus to recommendations for the Christian life-style, and result in the institutional and practical denial or domestication of Jesus' message and intentions.

Given our propensity to dualistic thought, it should come as no surprise to learn that one of the most vexing problems in modern physics is how to model, account for, or otherwise imagine and understand the wave-particle features of light. Light behaves as both particle and wave—not either/or. Likewise, the structures of reality seem to be forcing recent physics to put together what previously had been thought of as separate—space and time become space-time, matter and energy become matter-energy.

Is it any wonder that we are surprised to discover that other religions and cultures do not think dualistically? In his exposition of Zen Buddhism, the late Roshi Shunryu Suzuki wrote, "For Zen students the most important thing is not to be dualistic."[8] In the introduction to the volume, Richard Baker writes, "The editing is further complicated by the fact that English is profoundly dualistic in its basic assumptions and has not had the opportunity over the centuries to develop a way of expressing non-dualistic Buddhist ideas, as has Japanese." English is not alone among Western languages in this dualistic propensity. The entire West is dualistic in its discourse. Compare the profound, nondualistic statement made by the Dalai Lama of Tibet: "When it comes to loving, there are neither means nor ends, for loving is its own end." He indicated that he made the statement as one that Buddhists could make with Christians and Jews. I agree. But can the dualistic, Western mentality begin to comprehend the profound nature of the statement? Means and ends become one in the act of loving. How can that be?

Mechanism

Mechanism should not be difficult to understand as an attribute of the modern consciousness. Following Descartes and Newton, we view the world as a machine governed by immutable laws that can be understood by science and translated into mathematics. The machine includes the human as well, and the advent of modern social science carried the investigation into the arena of the mechanics of the human species.

The popular slang expression "If it ain't broke don't fix it" is applied to every aspect of our orientation to culture, from management to gardening. All things can be analyzed in terms of their respective mechanics and fixed or not fixed according to the diagnosis. When problems arise, from a declining social club to government itself, we set to work with our diagnostics to fix the contraption that is the club or government. Mechanistic diagnostics has transformed our world into an endless series of clanking mechanical constructs and images. It can be argued as well that it is the root assumption of mechanistic diagnostics that drives the seemingly endless stream of "how to" literature gushing from the presses these days. We purchase books that tell us how to diagnose and fix everything from business to our own spiritual lives, and the easier the diagnostic process given and the quicker the fix, the more popular the item on the market. In the process of the diagnosis we employ another essential ingredient of our temperament, reductionism.

Reductionism

We must reduce the machine to its simplest elements in order to understand the inner workings of the whole. That which is alive must be killed and reduced to nonreducible parts so as to understand how the whole functions as a machine.

Reductionism became an attribute of biblical and theological scholarship in the nineteenth-century Protestant liberal movement. The Scriptures, doctrines, and ethic of Christianity were reduced to their essential elements in order to diagnose and understand them and Christianity itself. An example of such mentality is the title of a famous book of the modern era, *Das Wesen des Christentums,* by Adolf von Harnack. The title means literally "the essence of Christianity."[9] Commenting upon the volume, theological historians John Dillenberger and Claude Welch wrote: "As the title of the work indicates, von Harnack proposes to delineate what is truly essential to Christianity—to get behind the externals, to strip off the husk and lay bare the kernel.[10] What is important to notice is the methodology of reductionism operative in such scholarship, that is, the reduction of Christianity to essential, nonreducible parts.

The German universities where von Harnack taught played out the reductionist game by splitting apart and reducing all areas of learning into *Wissenschaften,* or exact sciences. With that the modern notion of distinct academic disciplines was born, each but a single area of focus, methodology, and diagnosis. This approach pervades higher education today and is reduced or refined further by the notion of specialization as the principal avenue of education. "Finding the right person for the job" means finding the one who has reduced learning to the particular area of focus in question. Alfred North Whitehead observed that such thinking produces in education a "celibacy of the intellect" that succeeds in producing "minds in the groove."[11] Radical specialization can be reduced to the amusing, if not to the downright absurd. I will not soon forget a recommendation letter from a graduate school for a young candidate to our faculty. The candidate was defended with the statement "One must remember that one cannot be 'all things to all men' in the field of paleobotany."

Wedding reductionism and mechanism in the modern consciousness means that the appreciation for the organic connectedness of the whole of reality is lost. The woods cannot be seen for the trees. We think the whole is to be understood through the parts and not the other way around. However, for most of its history, humankind has not shared this view and methodology. And other contemporary cultures do not unless and until they are dominated by the West.

Certainly, the advent of environmental science and the new methods employed by naturalists who study creatures within their own environments represent important and healthy departures from this mechanistic-reductionist methodology that dominates modern thinking and investigation. What is new in these new methods is the assumption driving them that everything is connected to everything else. Thus, it is the appreciation of the connections and relationships within the totality of reality that presents us with a new image of the biosphere as a dynamic, interactive ecology.

Materialism

At its fundamental level, materialism means viewing the world as made of matter, or matter-energy, as the new physics would say. A striking example of the implications of this type of thinking arose from Descartes' insistence that the animal world was material in nature and did not share sentient mentality with us.[12] He insisted that "the greatest of all prejudices we have retained from infancy is that of believing that brutes think." Thought, for Descartes, distinguished the human from the nonhuman. The world of nature, viewed as unfeeling and unthinking matter, may be investigated, exploited, manipulated, and despoiled without reverence for its own nonmaterial, intrinsic value. Is it surprising, then, that agriculture and research often brutalize animals?

Descartes' materialism, when combined with reductionism, leads inevitably to reducing thinking itself to the interaction of matter within the brain. Likewise, all "legitimate" thinking is to be limited to the impact of the five senses upon the brain—senses that can be reduced to the interaction of matter also. Trustworthy knowledge is limited to the stimulus of the five senses. Thus, mind comes to mean *material* brain, and any notion of a spirit or soul is wishful fabrication. Does this sound odd? It is the logical working out of the process of radical empiricism which is the foundation of much modern science and philosophy and limits knowledge to the sensually provable.

I have a philosopher friend who once claimed to be an empiricist. One day he announced he was no longer an empiricist or positivist. Why? He had caught himself while shaving recounting those things he could *not* think about that day which were "emotive, meaningless nonsense." "What were you thinking about at the time?" I asked. He had been thinking about how much he loved his wife and children. Emotive, meaningless nonsense! Radical empiricism carried to its logical end results in absurdity, and yet its spell has captured much of the modern mind-set.

I am convinced that at another level materialism reduces our values to material substance. That is, we view the human as an economic animal who accumulates material property as the logical extension of human identity. We are what we own. We enact laws to protect the material goods that give us our sense of identity. We must ask ourselves, What identity are we protecting?

Determinism

Since Descartes, science and philosophy have constructed the modern paradigm on the assumption that all things are determined causally by immutable laws and that the parts of anything determine the character of the whole. Moreover, determinism assumes that the effect of a particular cause *is certain*. A hammer to the thumb produces pain, not pleasure, thoughtful meditation, or lucid poetry. Pain is the *certain* effect of the cause (hammer to the thumb). Much science, technology, political and economic theory, and certainly the popular mind-set continue to assume certain, causal determinism as fundamental to all reality. This determinism, however, logically rules out the unexpected and freedom. Thus, the classic problem of determinism versus free will continues to plague the modern consciousness. The work in quantum physics has led to the discovery of an "uncertainty principle" operative in the structures of reality. I refer to this principle in Chapter 2, for it is one ingredient that begins to alter presuppositions of causal determinism in modern consciousness.

In theology, the Western emphasis upon determinism has existed for centuries. It certainly goes back to Augustine in the fifth century who, in his debates with Pelagius, constructed a doctrine of grace that made salvation determined exclusively and with utter certainty by God alone.[13] Pelagius had argued for free will, holding that there was a God-given capacity for good intrinsic to human nature, and thus the human could contribute to the process of salvation. For Augustine, on the other hand, salvation was determined by God alone (*Sola Gratia*), because humans are utterly corrupted by the sin of Adam and hence *determined* by "original sin." Debates in the Middle Ages sought a compromise between these two positions. Nevertheless, determinism had already intruded with enormous impact and could not be put away. During the Reformation, Augustinian radical determinism surfaced. Divine determination of creation, predestination, even determination of individual life were notions planted deep in Protestant minds. In the eighteenth century, post-Reformation deism was thoroughly deterministic in its idea of the divine creator as a clockmaker who created the clock (i.e., creation) and set it to ticking according to the predetermined mechanical workings within its structure. Current fundamentalist Christian views of creation (creationism) and of the apocalyptic end of the world and second coming of Christ (millenarianism) are permeated with determinism.

What should concern us about the pervasiveness of determinism in Western consciousness—especially in its theological forms—is that with its denial of freedom and the unexpected comes the denial of ethical responsibility. Put most simply, if things are going to happen inevitably and we have not the ability to respond and alter the course of history, why should we bother to do anything? The best we can do is wait, "have faith," or immobilize ourselves with drugs or other means of escape in order to blot from consciousness the inevitable. Determinism extracts the moral nerve from humankind. It makes a mockery of ethics and should constitute our principal quarrel with any religion or political or economic policy of the "far right," for such a perspective does not allow the kind of responsibility, creativity, and novelty that ethical sensitivity requires. The determinism embedded within them presents us with the view that we are helpless before inevitable forces.

Individualism

Individualism does not seem to have been known among ancient peoples, but since the seventeenth century we have fostered the idea of the isolate, independent individual. Theologian-ethicist John Cobb has demonstrated that the idea of the independent individual posited by Hobbes and Locke was a myth, because the postulate set forth the notion that "each individual or household was independent of all others" as these individuals existed originally in a *hypothetical* "state of nature."[14] From the postulate was then developed a social theory that attempted to prove the inability of the individual or household to form a constructive society without benefit of monarchy (Hobbes) or social contract (Locke). Robert Bellah reminds us that such postulates "owed little to either classical or biblical sources."[15] Rather, the idea of the independent individual existing in a state of nature prior to any social order was a radical break with tradition and represented a new myth introduced into the Western mentality, and the myth produced the social theories extant in the West today. But there never existed such "independent individuals" in a "state of nature" prior to social organization. The whole idea is a hypothetical fabrication, a myth.

What power this myth has exerted in Western consciousness! It has made us fundamentally deny our deep, intrinsic sociality. The myth informs us that we are alone in the world and that social organization is just an agreement we reluctantly enter into in order to mitigate possible conflict of interest with other individuals. It explains that without the agreement we would be in a constant state of war with other isolate individuals and families. And, as Bellah reminds us again, the existing image of the lone cowboy hero in popular culture runs counter to the deep sociality that has always been intrinsic to human nature.[16] The myth fosters privatism and deludes us into the "wishdream" of being totally independent one day like the cowboy hero.

The myth of individualism supercedes all the ethical systems in the modern world with an ethic that really drives the institutions of modern society. Our ethical posture is one of defense and competition—defense of the individual against the onslaught of other individuals, and competition with other individuals in order to gain security, power, and enjoyment as one's own. The ethics of the myth operated in the development of modern economic theories. Defense and competition rule at the deepest levels of our consciousness over any ethical system one may advance in modern perspective.

Were it not so serious a problem, one could find amusing the ceremony and bombast that accompany the formulation of "business ethics," "congressional ethics," "investment ethics," and even "academic ethics." We pin the notice containing the new rules to the wall of the office and then go on as before with our competitive enterprises. When someone is caught breaking the rules, much ceremony and utter seriousness attend our indictment of the culprit, although all know the real failing of the villain was that greed outstripped caution and he or she was caught. Let us hope he or she does not ever do it again—so obviously. The villain is an embarrassment that leads to the deep, unavoidable premonition that our prisons are actually mirrors reflecting the deeper reaches of human consciousness. The wise longshoreman-philosopher Eric Hoffer once remarked that every time he hears of a criminal caught "I look within and discover the same culprit lurking."

The myth of individualism creates an ethical posture that tells us that sociality and cooperation are impossible, if not downright evil. With that, we assume hostile postures as nations against nations. Individualism sets a cold war mentality in cement. We imagine a world with lines drawn upon it separating peoples and nations, rather than the world as seen from space. And, to our detriment, Jesus' injunction to love our enemies so that we may be like God is never taken seriously.

Anthropocentrism

Anthropocentrism (from the Greek *anthropos*, meaning "man"), the concept that human beings are the center of all significant concerns, rules supreme in the modern consciousness. For example, when we read John 3:16 ("God so loved the world . . ."), we read "God so loved humans . . ." into the text. Although this is not necessarily contrary to the context of the passage, we automatically think of the world from an anthropocentric perspective. "World," for us, means "humans." But given the dangers in the world today, we must begin training ourselves to read the text as it is written: "God so loved the *world*." We must begin to ponder implications beyond the human sphere.

In keeping with this, John Cobb concluded a discussion of the environmental crisis with a critique that illustrates my thesis here.[17] Cobb shows that anthropocentric ethical systems of the modern world cannot help us do anything about the ecological crisis because our concerns are for the sake of human survival alone. We feel no kinship with the natural world and do not give serious consideration to the intrinsic value and survival of nature itself. We manipulate nature for *our* ends alone. It does not dawn upon our consciousness that the biosphere may have intrinsic value in and of itself, or that it might save us. No, we are in charge. We will save ourselves by mastering it. Now and again, as during an earthquake, nature reminds us that it is in charge, and we are but a dependent part of its structure.

Patriarchalism

An ancient, symbolic, and metaphorical mind-set has continued with us into the modern consciousness that has enormous theological, as well as social, implications. It is *patriarchalism*. The symbolic and metaphorical underpinnings of our mind-set are male oriented through and through, and feminist literature is demonstrating conclusively how such a habit of mind diminishes both sexes as well as our perceptions of reality.[18] With such an orientation, the isolate individual becomes estranged and removed from the opposite sex. At the deepest level, one becomes estranged from one's own true nature, which contains the opposite sexuality. The splitting apart of all perceived reality reaches to the deepest level of human consciousness and informs us that we are split asunder to the very core. Here we can see how modern thinking has built into itself the seeds of its own impoverishment and self-denial. That is, we deny or attempt to deny the other sexuality in ourselves at great psychological cost.

Deus ex Machina

Our thinking is dualistic, mechanistic, reductionistic, materialistic, and deterministic. It makes for a world of isolated individuals, groups, and nations. It is human centered and sustains the patriarchal splitting of reality to the very core of being. The question remains, What of God in such thinking? I know of no better critique of modern theological thought than Dietrich Bonhoeffer's observations, written in a Nazi prison.[19] With the rise of the modern temperament, Bonhoeffer noted that God was separated, or edged out, of the world of human perception into the gaps—the fringes of human experience. God became the *deus ex machina* (a god from a machine), a concept from classical antiquity that referred to a device used by playwrights to bring a god onto the stage in order to solve the problems of the plot. God, according to Bonhoeffer's analysis, is employed as such a device on the edge of human experience when perception and knowledge run to the end of their tether. There, where the gap appears, God is employed as a working hypothesis, as the solution—the answer. Thus, in the center of daily life, where consciousness reigns secure, humans live *etsi deus non daratur* (as if there were no God). But when things run to the end of their tether, call in the *deus ex machina!* Such a God becomes the God of human weakness, on the fringes of experience, not the God in the center of life. God becomes a God removed, beyond, utterly transcendent.

Bonhoeffer observed how the churches reacted in such a situation. They attempted to prove to people that they were weak and powerless in the center of life, to "call them back into their sin," thereby making them religiously feel the gap and the need for the *deus ex machina* at the center (what he called a "priestly snuffing about in the sins of man in order to catch them out"). Such tactics, he observed, were contrary to the way of Jesus, who called people out of their sins, not into them. Furthermore, he concluded that the whole enterprise was "pointless" and "ignoble." "Pointless, because it seems like an attempt to put a grown-up person back into adolescence. . . . Ignoble, because it amounts to an attempt to exploit human weakness."[20] Accordingly, Bonhoeffer sought a God in the center of human experience who was not a *deus ex machina*, not merely a clever device for priests and preachers.

Where Do We Go from Here?

What then is wrong with modern thinking? It can make us estranged from God, from nature, from the opposite sex, and from our own corporeal and spiritual capacities. It can make us environmentally suicidal and spiritually and ethically impotent. It can turn our notions of truth into illusions founded upon absurd images, myths, and fabrications. It can cut us off from appreciating, celebrating, reverencing, and loving the fundamental fact of reality we face daily—the elementary blessing of being alive in a universe that is brimming with fellow-life. It can cast us upon the shore of a lonely, deserted island where we swallow the bitter pill of self-denial and hatred.

This worldview can be especially destructive when held tenaciously to govern all thinking on all subjects. To be sure, some distinctions are necessary for clarity and logical procedure (dualism). Some things are by nature mechanical or may be understood according to mechanical models (mechanism); some may be reduced to their parts to aid understanding (reductionism); and others are best understood as having nonliving, material properties (materialism). Some things are determined according to a strict and certain causality (determinism); certain circumstances do set the individual alone (individualism); some issues exclusively involve humans (anthropocentrism); and some dimensions of life are male oriented (patriarchalism). Some, but not all! If we attempt to pack the whole of reality into the confines of this way of thinking, we delude and diminish ourselves. Thus, to call for a "new way of thinking" does not mean total abandonment of the modern way of thinking. Rather, it means recognizing its limitations and pressing for the expansion of our horizons. I conclude, in the last analysis, that Albert Einstein, Benjamin Reist, Joseph Sittler, and a host of others say that we must expand our horizons and move beyond this limited way of thinking, else we perish, and with us goes the earth that has nurtured us for so long.

But how do we unlock the confines of the modern worldview and expand our horizons? Can we make such an adjustment in thinking and action in time—before that crucial, environmental hour-of-no-return has arrived when it will be too late for thought of any kind? Can Christians make such an advance? Indeed, can Christian faith serve as an inventive resource and provide leadership in prompting such a monumental advance for the human species? We turn now to a serious and urgent consideration of these questions.

FOR DISCUSSION

1. Can you think of ways any of the isms mentioned here manifest themselves in your own thinking or life? How do these manifestations make you feel? What do they prompt you to think about your world?

2. In what ways do you think we are related to nature? In what ways do we disassociate ourselves from nature? What happens to nature in the process?

3. Of the various isms noted here that make up modern thinking, which would you isolate as being especially destructive or offensive for persons and for nature? Which of the isms would you classify as being "unchristian" or "unbiblical" in character? Which are necessary for modern life as we know it?

4. What are examples of the use of the *deus ex machina* in the church? In what ways do Christians live as if there were no God?

5. If you could create the best possible environment for yourself, what would it be like? How might others—people and creatures—be related to it? What would be needed to create such an environment?

2

POSSIBILITIES AND PERSPECTIVES FOR A NEW WORLDVIEW

Is it possible to put the destructive aspects of the modern way of thinking behind us? What could produce a constructive, new consciousness in us? Certainly, a trauma can alter the way we view life. We lose a pet during childhood and are set to asking new questions about life and death. A sudden illness, the loss of home or job, an accident—all such "catastrophes" can place us on a new track.

I have a colleague, with whom I have discussed the enormity of the global environmental problem, who argues convincingly that the *only* thing that will alter the current crisis will be a world catastrophe. He hopes it will be economic in character, because we could recover from such a human catastrophe while the biosphere remains relatively untouched. On the other hand, a nuclear exchange between the great powers, nuclear meltdowns in a host of reactors at the same moment, radical weather alteration caused by our tinkering with the atmosphere, large-scale pollution of farmlands, or poisoning the root of the biospherical food chain in the oceans would all be catastrophes that would so alter the nature of the biosphere itself that subsequent alteration of our thinking would be unable to avert the destruction of life on earth. I am forced to acknowledge the truth in what my friend argues. Nevertheless, the prospect it offers is so grim that I urgently search for other ways out.

Change undertaken through fear, however, is ephemeral. Gandhi was wise in declaring that "what is gained through fear lasts only while the fear lasts."[1] So how do we find a way out? Must fear of catastrophe be our only alternative?

Recall that the modern way of thinking discussed in Chapter 1 represents our underlying perception of the nature of reality. An important question to ask, then, is, Is reality *actually* what we conceive it to be in the modern worldview? If the answer is a clear and irrefutable no, then we are challenged to look for other ways to understand reality. But the answer may come to us less clearly, as little more than one idea among the many ideas that the intellect ponders without certain resolution. Resolute action and change in life-style would not follow from such an idea alone. The idea would have to penetrate to the heart and affections and become more than an intellectual construct. It would have to grip us at the core of our being or psyche if we are to be changed.

The Basis for a New Consciousness

Scholars representing disciplines as diverse as religion, philosophy, the natural and social sciences, art, literature, and agriculture have begun jointly to explore the nature of the modern consciousness and the prospect of there being an alternative postmodern consciousness.[2] Philosopher Fredrick Ferré has observed that those who represent what are thought of as independent disciplines are now acknowledging and exploring a theme and the resulting questions that posit the flow of thought from a modern to a postmodern worldview. The vision glimpsed is in fact a new worldview, or way of thinking, that is so novel that it challenges every canon of modernity. In fact, it is important to note that the postmodern worldview cannot be thought of as the exclusive province of any single science or discipline. Indeed, the new vision ultimately makes the notion of independent disciplines obsolete because it says no to the tendency of modern thought to split everything into independent units. It calls a halt to the operative principle of separation.

I explore in this and the following chapters the theological and ethical implications of the postmodern consciousness. But first, it is important that we reflect on the issue of a change in consciousness. Books, articles, and conference papers do not necessarily alter the way we view our world or act ethically in it. Such books, articles, and papers have no impact until they articulate a vision we already sense or hold at profound levels of our being. That vision must become a "catastrophe" for our modern thinking—an *inner catastrophe*, an inner lightning bolt that burns out an old, limited vision and replaces it with a new, more comprehensive one. Until and unless such an inner change occurs, we will turn away from the best-intended writings and ideas unmoved, unchanged.

Paul Tillich indicated with his usual clarity and precision the nature of the moral act. He wrote:

> A moral act is not an act in obedience to an external law, human or divine. It is the inner law of our true being, of our essential or created nature, which demands that we actualize what follows from it. And an antimoral act is not the transgression of one or several precisely circumscribed commands, but an act that contradicts the self-realization of the person as a person and drives toward disintegration.[3]

An "external" law, idea, or command is not likely to take hold in us and produce action. Only that which we perceive as being true to our own intrinsic nature can produce commitment, change, and action. Tillich here follows in the tradition of Plato and the prophets of Israel, who spoke of the same inner truth. Tillich goes on in his writings to show how Jesus also taught with such a perception in mind. Jesus' ethic is the depiction of himself, and thereby the depiction of what is best in and intrinsic to all human nature. Because of that inner truth, his teachings have had a powerful and lasting influence on human history.

This point has enormous implications for education. To impose upon people a teaching that they perceive as external or as inappropriate to their own nature can never elicit allegiance, commitment, and lasting, consistent action. To tell someone to believe and do something because "I say so," or "the church says so," or "government says so," or "God says so" is invariably seen as irrelevant, is resented for what it is, and is rejected. But a teaching that is perceived as being true to one's own being, and thus to reality as felt and known, will produce change, commitment, and action.

Thus, to recognize that the new vision is internal—already embedded in us and in reality itself—means that it moves beyond idea and beyond external opinion, and finds root in what we actually are and can become. Such a vision will change people, their actions and policies, and their orientation to the environment. Nothing short of this will do any good.

Contrary to the prospect of change accomplished through fear or ideas alone, an inner truth suggests the image of a "blessing" already embedded within us and may be seen as a lure that draws us on to internal growth. Matthew Fox cites the axiom of psychotherapist Frederick Perls that "the organism does not move by will, but by preference."[4] Naming the "blessing-lure" embedded within us as "preference" will mean naming the vision that may be new to our perception of reality as moderns, but not new to our deepest natures as children of the earth. It was always the aim of Pierre Teilhard de Chardin to demonstrate that this lure, or attraction, was inherent in evolution itself, was implicit in us, and was manifest organically in the incarnation in Jesus of the cosmic Christ, who is the Omega point, the destiny of the Creator's handiwork. It is this fact that makes the Christ appealing. Thus, Christ may be called the "lure" that the Creator places before us and within us to encourage our growth. For too long the churches have failed to follow through on the implications of this positive Christological notion concerning the potentials in human nature. Rather, as I began to argue in Chapter 1, they have removed the Christ from us, identifying him as a supernatural perfection beyond human nature. Christ became, thereby, an external reality, not the *inner truth* of human nature.

The Impact of Science

What might be the characteristics of the new vision, its new way of thinking, and its attendant new images of the nature of reality? What I intend is to elucidate it by investigating how this vision has been slowly emerging in the consciousness of many. In addition, it is worthwhile to note its origins and development in Western culture.

In the late nineteenth century, some Protestant liberal theologians began taking seriously the methodology and content of modern science, and began adapting these methods and content to their own enterprises. However, most Christians maintained a long-standing hostility toward the sciences, and science was indifferent to what Christians did or did not think about scientific enterprise. These tendencies carried over into the twentieth century.

Now, however, an unexpected turn has been taken by theologians representing a broad spectrum of Christian opinion and by many scientists as well. Mutually enriching discussions are occurring between theologians and scientists.[5] For example, physicists and biologists conversant with theology are writing books with theologians or are themselves writing books about science and theology. Theologians are writing of the impact of science upon their reflection and are conducting conferences on scientific topics, with many leading scientists participating enthusiastically. To be sure, not all theologians or scientists welcome this exchange, but it is receiving enough attention to warrant serious consideration.

There is not space here to detail the fruitful exchanges, but certain directions in the discussion are important to consider, and from them we may grasp the new images of reality they present.

Biology

The first is in the area of biology, specifically, the theory of evolution. Although biologists are still engaged in debate and exploration of the *processes* of evolution, theologians follow their work with interest because of their acknowledgment of the *fact* of evolution. Benjamin Reist, for example, writes: "If with Polanyi, and mindful of Pierre Teilhard de Chardin and the contemporary Australian biologist Charles Birch, we think of evolution as a 'feat of emergence,' we must take seriously the fact that it is still going on—it is not yet decided." He concludes that "on this side of the breakthrough associated with Darwin's work, faith can only confess its belief in God the Creator if God is still creating."[6] As evolution continues, so God's creating continues, which means that theology shifts its emphasis from the old image of a Creator establishing things once and for all, long ago, to a new image of a Creator still engaged in the process of creating.

This shift in emphasis does a most important thing. It calls into question the deterministic doctrine of creation that led to the clockmaker theory of the Deists and the deterministic doctrine of the fundamentalists (i.e., creationism), which removed God from current natural processes and, therefore, obviated Christian interest in nature. The imagination may move from seeing a God removed to seeing a God still intimately involved with the natural process. Many designate this shift, with its change in terminology about God, a shift from *theism* to *panentheism*. Matthew Fox writes:

> Now panentheism is not pantheism. Pantheism, which is a declared heresy because it robs God of transcendence, states that "everything is God and God is everything." Panentheism, on the other hand, is altogether orthodox . . . for it slips in the little Greek word *en* and thus means, "God is in everything and everything is in God."[7]

The addition of *en* (in) underscores the fact that in God we continue to live and move and have our being, because God continues to work creation in us. God is not the God removed, on the fringe of human existence, in the gaps depicted by Dietrich Bonhoeffer's analysis of modern theology. God is dynamically near at hand, at the very "ground of our being" (Tillich). And, after a lengthy discussion of modern science, physicist Harold Schilling can move into the area known as "process theology" and write:

> Furthermore, process thought enlarges on this principle [eschewing dualisms] by denying the traditional duality of the natural and the supernatural, and thus the complete separation between God and the world. This makes room for the biblical idea that God is in the world, while at the same time it is in him, an idea that represents panentheism rather than conventional theism.[8]

Another example of this shift in thinking is biochemist Arthur Peacocke's citing with favor the statement of mathematician D. J. Bartholomew that "the Being of God includes and penetrates the whole universe, so that every part of it exists in Him, but . . . that his Being is more than, and is not exhausted by the universe ('pan-en-theism')."[9] So Peacocke calls for a new theological emphasis upon God's immanence and the doctrine of *creatio continua* on grounds of the new biology, chemistry, and thermodynamics. This from a biochemist!

Physics and Relationality

The second area of discussion involves theologians and physicists, beginning with Einstein, who are discovering new views of a dynamic and evolving universe. Newton's static machine is giving way to the concept of a dynamic universe in process. A crucial element in this new, dynamic view of reality is summarized by theologian Paul Knitter:

> Reality was no longer seen as a well-ordered machine, made up of discrete parts neatly linked to each other. Rather, it was a buzz of activity, of constant process, in which the parts could not even be neatly determined and located. At its deepest, subatomic level, the world did not seem to show any "basic building blocks" or "beings," but rather an intricate, ever changing, and interrelating process of activity or becoming.
>
> It was especially the new physics that prompted philosophers to a further insight into the way things are: if everything is a becoming rather than a being, the becoming takes place through *interrelating*. If we can be only if we become, we can become only if we reach out and relate. Nothing, whether an electron or a human being, can be "an island unto itself."[10]

This view of relationality as the ground of the processive nature of all reality was a basic presupposition in the thinking of philosopher Alfred North Whitehead and in the development of what is called "process theology." Thus, "relationality is prior to process, since it generates it."[11] Recall that the myth of individualism discussed in Chapter 1 tells us that we are distinct, isolate beings prior to contact and relationship. The new view of science demonstrates that just the opposite is the case. We become ever and again events or occasions of individuation through relationships, and this process is endless.

To put this another way, modern thought has been governed by the static noun, whereas postmodern thinking is to be governed by the active verb. Any attempt, therefore, to isolate and define ourselves, the world, or its creatures in static terms is as futile as attempting to mark a bird in flight, because from the subatomic level to its galactic dimensions all reality is a dynamic process of becoming through interrelationships. Description and biography are more appropriate to reality, therefore, than are static definition and systematic or creedal proposition.

Explorations into Einstein's general and special relativity theories, his work in quantum physics, and the quest for what is called the "unification theory" of all reality related to "super symmetry" all present questions with great theological implications. Exploring these scientific theories and their theological implications in detail is not my intent here. But one area of discussion between some theologians and scientists is the view of a Creator at work from the subatomic level to the vast expanse of the galaxies. This view suggests a Creator operating with love. Physicist Harold Schilling summarizes the view by saying:

> Thus, God affects the behaviour of other entities not by force, in a mechanical sense, but by what may by analogy be called persuasion, or a luring on, or loving guidance.[12]

Such a vision is thoroughly in keeping with the emphasis in Scripture on both a God of love and the Covenant God. Covenant, of course, implies relationship, which seems to be the very ground of the process of creation itself. All of this obviously challenges the notion of God as the *deus ex machina* discussed earlier. The implication of this revisionist thought is that interrelationship, novelty, and creative love characterize the Creator's way with creation—not domination and force of power.

Physics—Quantum Theory

The third new direction of discussion assumes that the idea of certain, causal determinism has also been challenged by the work of Heisenberg and those physicists working in quantum theory. Physicists are beginning to construct models and employ methods that acknowledge the fact that physical reality includes remarkable novelty and uncertainty. In many cases this means that causes may produce a range of probable effects rather than precise, certain effects. As physicist-theologian Ian Barbour writes: "The future is not simply unknown, it is 'not decided'; but it is not completely 'open,' since the present determines the range of future possibilities."[13]

It is interesting to note that some scholars, in attempting to portray vividly the complex field of quantum physics, turn to Eastern religion and philosophy to explain their science.[14] My own view is that they do this because strict causal determinism has so dominated our philosophical and theological thinking that analogies appropriate to quantum physics are lacking in the West. However, the important point to grasp is that scientists are leading theologians away from strict, causal determinism toward a world of the unexpected and evolutionary theory. With that comes interest once again in what I would call the "preferential referent of nature"; that is, all thought must now relate to nature if it is to be cogent and relevant. Christianity cannot continue to ignore nature as it has done since Augustine's argument that the study of nature contributes nothing to our appreciation of salvation. Nor can Christianity ignore the inextricable link between ourselves, God, and nature. The separated modern universe is being replaced with a postmodern worldview that encompasses all things as dynamically connected. Arthur Peacocke observes that this presents us with a new form of Christian "materialism," because it makes for "a way of relating the physical and personal worlds that avoids any stark dichotomy between them, seeing them rather as two facets of the same reality."[15]

Often I ask my theology students, "Where can one point and say, 'God'?" The question usually meets with silence. Scientists and theologians are beginning to point to nature itself, to cosmic history, and to us all, who share in the process of emergence as significant clues to the character of the Creator on the move and at work. Arthur Peacocke is so bold as to make the case that "in a human being (or beings) the presence of God the Creator might be revealed with a clarity not hitherto perceived." This means that "the more personal and *self*-conscious the entity in which God is immanent, the more capable it is of expressing God's supra-personal characteristics."[16] In this light we may appreciate how God is able to be known through the man Jesus, who was open to

God and thereby open to being the agent of a remarkable revelation of the immanent God. Not only is that the case with Jesus, but it is suggestive of a unique capability of all humans as self-conscious beings. All humans can be agents of revelation because God is immanent in them!

This view of God's revelation through a person or persons does not need to entertain the dualistic notions of natural and supernatural substance employed by the authors of the ancient creeds. Panentheism presents us with God's immanence in a new way. God is already in all things and in all peoples. Revelation, therefore, breaks through human consciousness and does not require a change or admixture of substances or natures. Rather, it requires an openness and sensitivity of consciousness to what is already present, that is, to God, because that consciousness is already in God.

But, are we linked inextricably, as I said earlier, with nature, with evolution, and thereby with the immanent Creator's handiwork? Astronomy and physics are providing irrefutable evidence that we are linked at the subatomic level to the forces unleashed with the Big Bang, the fireball that was the origin of all things billions of years ago. For instance, with a supernova, the explosion of a star, comes the production of heavy elements that make possible the calcium in living bone and the chemistry of living blood. We are linked. The expanding universe is our home. In it we live and move and are becoming. And because our "home" is *in* the Creator (panentheism), we are in God and God is in us. To deny that fact is to suffer a delusion—a false image—that places us back in the destructive anthropocentrism of the modern worldview.

We are just beginning to comprehend the enormous and far-reaching implications these new views have for theology and science. A host of new notions present themselves for consideration, ranging from ecology, evolution, processive reality, uncertainty, creativity, and novelty, to panentheism and immanence. These new ideas alter radically old notions of reality, provide new insights into the Scriptures, and trigger the imagination to grasp the structures of reality in radically new ways. The new biology and physics have given new contours to theological discussion, and theology is awakening to an utterly new agenda because it is awakening to a new view of all reality.

Most certainly, the view of our Creator that begins to dawn upon the imagination as we take all these new currents of scientific thought seriously is staggering. Indeed, God is powerful and all knowing in wisdom. Just look at the universe! But this powerful and inexpressibly wondrous Creator is above all else loving and gentle. God lures rather than controls, provides novel occasions for change and invention. God is creative beyond imagination. Just consider the complexities of reality at all levels and the possibilities for emergence that have in fact already emerged. For example, science has discovered 300,000 different species of beetles. That is emergence! And we are now told by science that this universe may not be the only one extant. God is a risk-taker. The range of possibilities for the future remain open; and we most certainly are part of the risk involved, because beside the prospect of our good stands the equal prospect of our evil. God creates life at the most profound levels and with incredible complexity and beauty. God is one who wills the creative interrelationship of all things but whose will may be accomplished in billions of novel ways. God is intimately involved in everything that is happening; thus God knows and feels all that is happening. And to think Augustine attempted to convince the church it had nothing to learn from the study of nature!

Rediscovering the Creation-Centered Tradition

The other foundations set down for postmodern thought arise from discovering and reclaiming the worldview of the Scriptures. The discovery involves a unique thread of thought that runs from the ancient to the present world. It has survived the denials and dominance of Augustinian and Cartesian modes of thinking. Matthew Fox calls that thread the "creation-centered tradition." Its components are as follows:[17]

1. The creation-centered tradition begins with a world of bless-

ing and links all in continued blessing through the concept of God's creative energy (Hebrew, *dahbar*). This is in contrast to the Augustinian starting point of original sin and curse, which Jewish scholars say is not found in Genesis. For centuries Christian churches have been dominated by the gloomy reading of the creation stories of Genesis set forth by Augustine. Biblical scholarship is beginning to appreciate the sense of wonder and joy the ancient Hebrews experienced when considering the creation and the Creator. With that, the Hebraic awareness of creation as blessing challenges the Augustinian reading.

2. A cosmological perspective for understanding the place of humans in the world is in contrast to the individualism and anthropocentrism of modern thinking. I am certain that new scientific information that we are linked to the stars and thus to the origins of the universe would not have surprised or put off the ancient biblical writers. Likely they would have taken the news as elaboration of their insight that we are made of the dust of the earth.

3. There is a celebration of the natural and the spiritual as one, in contrast to a separation of the natural from the spiritual that leads much Western religion toward denial of the natural and toward asceticism. Ancient biblical writers do not denigrate the fact that our spirituality must be a spirituality as embodied, nature-filled creatures. Indeed, they celebrate the fact.

4. Humans are viewed as potentially destructive and are called out of their sin, in contrast to the view that humans are corrupted and in need of the *deus ex machina*. Humans are high and ennobling, in contradiction of much Christian doctrine.

5. Emphasis is given to the cosmic Christ that was manifest in Jesus the prophet who calls others to their own divinity, in contrast to the lack of the cosmic Christ in much of Christian thinking where emphasis is placed instead on Jesus as supernatural savior. Early Christians knew that what connected the Creator with the

lilies of the field was the cosmic Christ, the *Logos* of John's gospel (John 1:1–18), made incarnate in the man Jesus. It is the divine connectedness of all things by means of the cosmic Christ, the *Logos*, that is the point of such an emphasis. Thus, to injure the creature is to injure the Creator, and to love the creature is to love the Creator. Anthropocentrism is blind to the cosmological Christ because it is blind to the cosmos. Thus, when the *Logos* comes home, its own people do not receive it. They are blind to the connection. And in keeping with John 1:1–18, those who do receive the *Logos* are reconnected with the Creator. They are given to see all things in God. The creation is given over to them as blessing, for their eyes are able to see the connection between a loving Creator and a love-filled creation. Moreover, the *Logos* connects God and humans such that the divinity in humans may be affirmed.

6. Spirituality frees us from ideology, rather than from our senses and natural state. Growth and health in Christian life are measured by our openness to learning and our capacity to contribute lovingly to the expansion of life in all its dimensions, rather than by the drab attributes of a lifeless asceticism that denies the beauty inherent in life. The standards for assessing the value of one's life will ultimately be "Did I learn to love, and did I acquire knowledge?"[18] Implicit is the prospect for continuous growth in love and knowledge into eternity. And because learning of any kind requires pliant openness to confront courageously what is new, a spirituality that frees us of the block that is ideology makes for learning and suggests itself as a portent of eternal life.

7. An emphasis on cosmic healing and salvation that includes all of creation, including humans, is in contrast to an emphasis upon personal salvation alone, without reference to the rest of creation. The Creator blesses and loves all that has been made, and it behooves humans to emulate the Creator's blessing and love for all things because humans are called to be the covenant partners of God. Put bluntly, to pollute, disfigure, or harm the gift that is the earth is to spit into the face of the Creator. But to take joy in

the earth is to rejoice in God and to become like God, who takes joy in the creation. *NOT EXACTLY* *needs to explain language w/*

8. The Trinity is reaffirmed, with equal emphasis upon Father, Son, and Holy Spirit, as over against a tritheism that practices idolatry of the Son at the expense of Father and Holy Spirit. Accordingly, the view of God remains monotheistic. That is, it affirms in all truth that it is *one God* who creates (Father), who reconciles lovingly and calls us forward into our own spiritual and ethical potential (Son), and who transforms all life (Spirit); in contrast to the "pop-view" of a superstar Savior who leads believers to the great, judgmental white-bearded figure in the sky, while, close by, an enigmatic, sharp-eyed holy bird looks on.

The much-debated and often-misunderstood doctrine of the Trinity, which was implicit in the church's message from its earliest days, was a statement about monotheism. That is, it answered the question about the one God in three ways derived from human experience of the one God. I believe that four questions accompanied by four answers make clear what the doctrine attempts to express concerning all Christian experience:

QUESTION 1: Whom do we encounter in the life and ministry of the man Jesus of Nazareth?
ANSWER: We encounter a God who embraces us and all creation with love and compassion. It is a love and compassion willing to suffer with the creation and on behalf of the creation. Son and Logos are two names given to the character of this encounter. *Also Sophia — etc.*

QUESTION 2: Is this God, the God of Israel, also the creator of all things?
ANSWER: Yes. This is the Creator demonstrating to us the Creator's nature, which is love. With that we are given insight into the destiny of the creation itself, that is, the Creator's will lovingly to commune with the creation into eternity. Following Jesus' example, we name this God with the parental metaphor "Father." *Too limiting —*

QUESTION 3: Because these encounters with God, mediated

through Jesus and the history of Israel, occurred in the past, can we know this God now and in the future?

ANSWER: Yes. This God is now and ever present to our spirits as spirit, to our persons as mysterious personal presence, and to our subjectivity as holy subject. This presence is a transforming power that leads the creation into new life. We name this transforming presence "Holy Spirit."

QUESTION 4: Has our experience defined three gods or One God?

ANSWER: We have described three ways in which the One God is known to us: Creator, Compassionate Love, and Transforming Presence. As Christians, we declare Jesus of Nazareth to be the agent of this all-embracing revelation of the One God. Accordingly, we designate Jesus with titles such as Emmanuel (God with us), the Christ (the anointed one of God), Son of God (the first of a new generation of God's children), and Lord (the Lord of this new generation of beings, to whom, as Lord, has been given authority over all creation). In Jesus we encounter not only the One God, but also the ground, model, and destiny of humanity, which the One God has given us.

Although numerous writers and thinkers, artists and poets who have been part of the creation-centered tradition are found as far back as the book of Genesis, those on the list of the dominant tradition in the West do not even make it back to the New Testament! Rather, that list begins with Augustine in the fifth century! Recalling and reclaiming the older creation-centered tradition allows theologians to link in meaningful and inventive ways the thinking of postmodern science with the thought found in the Bible.[19] It would seem that the Judeo-Christian tradition is awakening from a long slumber with the aid of scientific as well as biblical and theological research.

The Postmodern Vision

What, then, constitutes the new, postmodern vision? Because it is a vision that we are only now beginning to recognize, it is difficult to be totally comprehensive or precise. Nevertheless, much can be suggested, if not delineated. What follows corrects the limitations of modern thought I described in Chapter 1 and should help us enrich our modes of thinking in a manner appropriate to the postmodern vision.

The postmodern orientation is holistic: it would have us expand our investigation by perceiving the whole, not just the parts. Also, it would have us see the parts in the light of the whole. This vision perceives, thereby, the inner connections and inner connectedness of all things. It seeks to bring together what modern thought has torn asunder, and therefore rejects mechanistic reductionism and sensate empiricism as the only avenues for investigation and knowledge. The postmodern vision makes room for other modes of perception and knowledge—intuition, for example, which is knowledge through the immediacy of participation in the thing known. Such a vision allows for knowledge at levels that transcend intellection. It values the heart and the imagination along with the intellect, for these deep levels of perception can teach us more than our language can express.

The new way understands that wisdom can transcend the making of distinctions by not insisting upon either/or, but by attempting to appreciate the dynamics of the whole that invariably includes both/and. Thus, it challenges our dualism by seeking to value relationships.

In religious thought, the postmodern vision does not deprecate the natural, the fleshly, the human, in favor of the spiritual, supernatural, and sacred. The spiritual in the natural is affirmed, along with the natural as the ground of the spiritual. Indeed, nature becomes sacred from this perspective, because it is the sphere wherein we sense the presence of the Creator. That, after all, is the meaning of the panentheistic insight in theology.

The new vision radically questions the general appropriateness of determinism and views reality as statistically uncertain or as characterized by probability. It values freedom and openness to the new. Reality is not reduced to the image of a "rigidly programed machine,"[20] but is seen as living, dynamic, organismic, and, above all, *processive* in character. It affirms that we live in a processing, changing, evolving universe in which the immanent Creator is at work—and play!

The new vision challenges us to shun radical materialism in the light of the perception of the world as alive at profound levels. The person becomes identified not with material objects, but with other humans, with other creatures, with the living wonder of the biosphere. It identifies with; it does not separate from. And with that, our infatuation with the myth of individualism is challenged. Neither is the new vision human-centered, but is what Matthew Fox calls "creation centered," recognizing our destructive capability but shunning destruction in favor of creation. It looks not to an apocalypse, but to beatitude. It is founded upon the deep perception that this world, this universe, this life is an inexpressible blessing, a glorious gift and treasure that requires respect and reverence.

The new vision is certainly not patriarchal, but affirms the female in the male and the male in the female. Thus, it maintains an openness to new metaphors that speak to the wholeness of our reality. It challenges us to appreciate the whole person. Patriarchalism, however, is so deeply embedded in us that it is not going to pass without great effort. One place to begin is with our language. A good exercise would be to begin altering perception by altering the language used to describe anything at the most basic level. Everytime you catch yourself using "he," "him," "she," and "her" regarding ideas, things, boats, buildings, or God, reverse genders in your speech. Our language can create images that can illumine and open up reality, or it can fix our reality in enclosed structures that are impervious to further thought.

Here we may be instructed by Sallie McFague's exposition of metaphor. She points out that all useful metaphors contain "two active thoughts which remain in permanent tension or interaction with each other." This means that two things both are and are not like what is named by the metaphor. For example, God *is and is not like* a father, and fathers *are and are not like* God. The usefulness of the metaphor is maintained only when the tension and interaction are maintained. Both things named by the metaphor are altered in our perception because of the interaction created. That is, both God and father are altered in our understanding by the interaction. McFague notes the importance of this in terms of religious models, "because the human images that are chosen as metaphors for God gain in stature and take on divine qualities by being placed in an interactive relationship with the divine."[21]

However, in taking a metaphor literally, the tension and interaction are lost, and one fails to understand what the metaphor is driving at. Prospects for the elaboration of thought are blunted, and nothing meaningful may be considered or said. If we say, for example, "She is sugar" and take the metaphor literally, then it may be inferred that she is sweet, white, granulated, and dissolves in water. Absurd! The enigmatic mystery of sweetness would not be comprehended in the way the metaphor intended.

It is in this light that we understand McFague's insight that "what is not named is not thought; symbol and concept go together and hence the form of the naming dictates the nature of the thought."[22] Name God "father" only, and we are stuck with father as image along with what the image suggests. If we name God father *and* mother, liberator, friend, lover, wooer, inventor, creator, artist, companion, or teacher, thought prospers.

Benjamin Reist adds to McFague's insight. He writes: "The world in which 'what is not named is not thought'—this indeed is the world in which theological idolatry can flourish." Especially is this the case when metaphors are taken literally, as when the father image for God suggests that God *is* a father, and not that God *is and is not like* a father. Thereby the mystery of God is lost in our appreciation, and God becomes the "He" who is the great, male white-bearded figure in the sky. Moreover, Reist adds that "the world in which 'the form of naming dictates the nature of the thought' must recognize that *if the form of naming is fixed, there can be no thought about the unexpected, the genuinely new.*"[23]

New ways of naming can make for new thinking and imaginative insight about God, people, the world. Openness to new naming can mean openness to what we may become, to what we are being challenged and lured by the Creator to become, that is, "after the measure of the stature of Christ." New naming can provide new insights as to what that measure and stature entail. New naming can mean openness to an evolving universe. New thought is possible, and thus new metaphors are possible. Obviously, no single metaphor can capture the whole of reality. But to insist upon already-received metaphors or to take them literally impoverishes our understanding, calls forth idolatry, and stops the evolution of human consciousness.

Christians are challenged to follow the example of Christ, who dislodged a theological mind-set of late Judaism by using the term *Abba* as a metaphor for God. *Abba* means Father in the most personal and familiar sense of the word. The metaphor brought God near at hand as a loving and caring parent. But the subsequent insistence on this metaphor and its literalization in much subsequent Christian thinking allowed patriarchalism to grow into a new idolatry theologically, institutionally, and socially. The expansion intended by the metaphor was blunted. With it, half the human race was elevated, and the other half became increasingly oppressed and seen as the so-called weaker sex, that is, less than divine. The parental and nurturing character of the Creator was lost to view, and both fatherhood and divinity were distorted.

Sallie McFague experiments with her own metaphors for God. Striking is her selection of the word *friend*. McFague does not call this or any metaphor a root metaphor for theology, however. She can be equally critical of "friend" as metaphor for God, underscoring her insistence that we be open to new metaphors and new insights because of the deeper recognition that the "root metaphor of Christianity is not any one model but a relationship that occurs between God and human beings."[24] Thus, many metaphors may be used, metaphors of relationship. Each points beyond itself to the deeper reality of the divine-human encounter. But our search for meaningful metaphors that model that encounter must extend beyond the human–divine to suggest the relationship between a creative God and an evolving universe, a relationship that includes all and connects all intimately.

The worldview I have been discussing is already within us, but it is new to our world today. It is with us because it is actually very old. It has existed in Western culture, but has been repressed,

denied, imprisoned, and punished. It has survived, seasoned with
the blood of martyrs. It has produced literature; it has thrived on
poetry and song. It still lives in us and will not be denied, because *what*
it represents the best that is in us all and affirms our true nature. *does*

A point essential to grasp is that there is no room in the *system*
postmodern worldview for a system of thought. Why? Because *of*
reality is dynamic and alive, changing, and on the move. A system *thought*
is static, contained, and closed. It cannot pretend to encompass *men?*
what is changing and dynamic. For that reason, the new worldview
requires thought that remains open-ended at the most profound
levels. For that reason it seeks perspective and vision in place of
system. With that perspective, that vision, it can change our way
of thinking, because new, dynamic images of reality are made
possible. For Christians this means that they may follow God into
a future where new life awaits a new thinking. They may do this
with faith and hope, for the creation reminds them daily of the
love of the Creator for all things—including themselves.

This new vision encourages us to cast our awful, modern solem-
nity to the winds and join what Thomas Merton called the "cosmic
dance" of the Creator and the creation.[25] Matthew Fox sees such a
dance not as a climb up an elitist, spiritual ladder, but as a dance
around "Sarah's circle." Fox notes that a circle dance is intrinsically
democratic and nonviolent for two reasons. First, one is eye to eye
with all others, "and if you have any sense of shared humanity at
all," you do not want to be the cause of the tears you can easily
see in the other's eyes. Second, in a circle there is a "built in
equalizer."[26] Another can do to you what you do to them!

With this we find a new social model for spirituality. Because
Merton insists on the *cosmic* dimensions of the dance with the
Creator, then, *a propos* Fox, we the dancers must be brought eye to
eye with every other creature on earth. From this perspective, Fox
argues, "an experience of cosmic awareness is a basic ingredient
for true compassion." He insists that in Hebrew thought, "love of
nature for its own sake distinguished true compassion from its
spurious, sentimental form." Indeed, "to fail to act out of our
kinship with all creation is to invite the brutality that narcissism so
easily entertains."[27] Thus, cosmological awareness of both the

Hebrew and the postmodern perspectives argues for anthropocentrism as the root of brutality and evil toward the Creator's handiwork. The ancient and new (postmodern) cosmologies provide theological ethics with a creation-centered, compassionate, blessing orientation.

This description of the new vision that can produce in us a new way of thinking obviously suggests more than I have said, and that is the way a vision should work. Its appropriate articulation must await new art and song. One thing is certain, those new songs will extol the earth and, thereby, the glory of the Creator.

Because the new theological emphasis I have discussed in this chapter is on the panentheistic, or immanent, God, the question persists: How does one really come to know this immanent God directly? In answer to that question, I will draw upon resources available within the biblical and Christian traditions.

FOR DISCUSSION

1. Can you enumerate ways in which you already share what has been called the "new worldview"? In what ways does it contradict your own thinking?

2. In what ways are we both male and female as humans? How might this change the way we live together?

3. Consider and discuss ways in which human life begins and ends with blessing. How is blessing a primary attribute of all life?

4. What customs, policies, doctrines, or thoughts block us from adopting the new consciousness? What might be done about such blocks? What habits of mind could we establish that would assist us in thinking in these new ways?

Part II

TOWARD A NEW
SPIRITUALITY AND ETHIC

3

A SPIRITUALITY TO TRANSCEND
MODERN LIMITATIONS

"Knowing" versus "Belief In"

The new word for it in colleges and seminaries is "spirituality." In the Middle Ages Christians knew it as "contemplation" (*contemplatio*). Often it has been called "mysticism." The 'it' in question has always meant the experimental science of deep prayer and meditation that is the root of religious experience, the core of monasticism, and is to be found in all of Christian tradition, with the possible exception of the recent fundamentalist tradition. That it is being reintroduced into the required studies of seminaries is a good sign, because a primary characteristic of the modern way of thinking is the denial of the mystic and, with that, the denial of the root of religious experience. The reintroduction of spirituality into the seminary curriculum cannot help but enlarge the range of theological awareness, and, above all, contribute to a deep appreciation of the postmodern way of thinking.

Every major world religion has a mystical component. Indeed, it may be argued that mysticism is the root of all religion. Isaiah 6:1–8 represents a classic mystical experience characteristic of the Hebrew prophets. The Old Testament Wisdom literature and the literature of the *kabbalah* of later Judaism have mystical components. Muhammed's mystical visions produced the canons of the Qur'an. Sufism and Baha'i are mystical branches of Islam. Ponder what Jesus was doing on those nights he went into the hills for prayer. I will argue that there are grounds for understanding Jesus' own self-consciousness, intentions, power, authority, and message in the light of what we know about Jewish and Christian mysticism.[1] And most certainly, Paul was a mystic.[2]

From the early Desert Fathers to the twentieth-century writings of Thomas Merton, mysticism has permeated Christian faith in the West. The Greek Orthodox mystical tradition, equal to if not richer than Western tradition, may be found embedded in the writings of the early Greek Fathers of the Patristic period, and gains focus in the rich treatments called the *Philokalia*, wherein the famous "Prayer of the Heart" is exposited for all Greek Orthodox Christians.[3] One need not argue that Asian religions are mystical in orientation or that Native American religions were and are mystical; their literature and practices make the case.

The word *spirituality* is of recent invention and is being adopted with zeal. So much is this the case that the word is quickly losing what denotational and connotational value it once possessed, and now stands for almost anything a religious group wishes to make it mean. The word *mysticism* has shared the same fate. The significance of the adoption of the word, however, represents the fact that the churches are awakening from the religious slumber produced by modern thought. Why this is happening reveals much concerning what spirituality is, as well as what the modern worldview is.

In Chapter 1 we saw that rational intellection and empiricism (perception through the five senses) were considered the only valid modes of perception and knowledge by those who produced, represent, and defend modern thinking. Spirituality—whether it be known as contemplation, mysticism, or another term—denies this limitation of human modes of perception. Spirituality holds that we can know more than either the senses or the intellect can teach us. It values what we call "intuition," but moves beyond intuition to a form of knowledge and awareness wherein the usual subject-object distinctions of knowledge break down entirely. There, by *participation in*, one comes to know that which is known. There one sees without benefit of eyes; one senses beyond the data and sensitivity of the five senses; one perceives with what the Hebrews called the "heart" (*lebab*). Indeed, it comes as a surprise to those oriented to modern science and philosophy to learn that the ancient Hebrews had no word for *mind*.[4] They used the word heart to mean the deep foundation that makes humans perceive, will, think, act, love, hate, and pray. Thinking, for them, meant the heart speaking quietly to itself in the depths.

Mystical, or contemplative, theology holds that deep perceptiveness does not teach us things *about* God and reality that we may then carry about as so much intellectual baggage or tuck away into a belief system within the mind. Rather, it teaches that it is possible to know God. To *know* rather than to know *about*. They are two very different things. Knowing God is a knowledge of the heart deep within the roots of perception, where one finds a certainty and clarity that does not escape the knower. Yet that knowledge does not lend itself to intellectual construction or precise and systematic verbal description and discourse. It is intuitive, immediate, participatory, and relational in character. The intellect comes into play after the fact of such knowledge or awareness and assists in "unpacking," as best it can, what is already known. This explains why the Scriptures of the world are filled with poetry, metaphor, and analogy, and why religion uses music and art to express what is beyond expression. This is why good theology always points beyond itself in its formulations. We "see through a glass darkly" (1 Corinthians 13:12), but we do *see!*

The modern mentality cannot tolerate these modes of mystical perception, which challenge and go against the canons of reason and empiricism and make a shambles of systematic discourse. They confuse precision, do not lend data for mathematical formulation, and otherwise wreak havoc with modern intellection. Is it any wonder that religion informed by modern thinking would deny the validity of mysticism? Theology has followed modern science and philosophy, and limits perception to rational thinking and empirical observation. With that, modern theology and piety, both conservative and liberal, have denied the foundations of faith and reduced faith itself to *belief in*—a rational process that usually means giving volitional and rational assent to propositions from the creeds. The relational, intuitive, and mystical dimensions of faith are neglected or denied.

In contrast, consider how we know the love of another person.

I am lucky to have had the experience in the Jesuits to teach me this fallacy!

Yes, there are empirical and rational dimensions to the knowing, but these are founded upon and expressive of deep relationship, intuition, and a perception that transcends intellect. Trying to prove to another that you love him or her is to limit your proof to empirical data and rational discourse. The result will be that the other person will *believe in* your love as a creed, a paragraph, a proposition, as analysis of data sketched on a graph. But he or she will not *know* your love. The person will *believe in it,* a very different thing indeed! Modern theology and piety have been teaching *belief in* for the past three hundred years or so under the modern worldview. The result is that, by denying its mystical roots, modern liberal theology has become bankrupt. And modern fundamentalists will not allow critical tinkering with the creeds because their God is a paragraph within the creed. Alter the words and the whole belief system collapses.

Several years ago I had a very conservative, fundamentalist Christian student who asked me, "Do you believe in Jesus Christ as your personal savior?" I decided to test his perceptiveness by formulating my answer in as many different ways as I could without using the words "Jesus Christ is my personal savior." And yet, my expressions meant the same thing. For example, I said, "I hold and trust that the man Jesus, who is the 'anointed one of God' (literal meaning of the word *Christ*), by means of his ministry and resurrection attested in the Scriptures, gives to humankind access to the redemptive and loving heart of the Creator, such that life may be transformed by the work of the Spirit of God now and into eternity." He thought a moment and then said, "So, you're not a Christian." I hadn't used the correct formula!

Mystical theology, or spirituality, provides a way back to our Judeo-Christian roots. With the return to those roots comes a rediscovery of the dimensions or characteristics that we have already seen contributing to the postmodern vision. Spirituality will be an important element in postmodern theological reflection and ethics. It can take the lead in expanding our horizons by showing us ways we can know more about reality than modern thought provides. How that is the case we must now consider in detail.

Spiritual Paths

It is more appropriate to speak of Christian spirituali*ties* than spirituality, for there are important differences among spiritualities. I would have us consider three principle types: neoplatonic, mundane, and creation-centered.

Neoplatonic Spirituality

Neoplatonic spirituality has dominated monastic life in the West. The Greek philosophers Plotinus and Proclus delineate a form of meditation wherein one "closed one's eyes" (*muo*) to all external things of the world in order to reach the "One" through deep contemplation.[5] This meant closing the external eyes so that the inner eye could be open to wisdom. Christians adopted this method in their quest for mystical union with God. Dionysius the Areopagite was such a neoplatonic Christian writer whose work became popular when translated into Latin by John Scotus Erigena (ca. 810–880). In addition, speculations on the "generation of the divine *Logos*" (Son of God) that were part of the debate leading to the formulation of the doctrine of the Trinity in the fourth century were couched in neoplatonic terms.[6] When combined with Augustine's fall/redemption model of Christian existence, neoplatonism dominated discussion of the processes of salvation.

The Greek philosophers posited the idea of a great "chain of being" extending from God to matter. Christian thinkers adopted the idea and from it drew a unique inference, which they depicted as a ladder. The lowest rung was material, the highest was spiritual; corresponding gradations lay between the two. To achieve monastic spirituality, one needed to scale the ladder, climbing from the material world to the spiritual.[7] The way devised for scaling the ladder was "purgation." Purgation meant asceticism (the denial of the flesh); its correlate, humility, was defined as self-renunciation. This type of spirituality was characterized by elitism. Those on the top rungs of the ladder were the spiritually elite. Such a writer as John of the Cross insisted that the highest reach of the purgative process is not for all Christians.[8] Becoming spiritual, then, came to mean denying the corporeal side of human nature, renouncing the world, and progressing through contemplation into a spiritual life, spiritual illumination, and union with God. Accordingly, the monastic setting was seen as the appropriate locus for reaching the top rungs of the ladder. The lowest rung was the condition of fleshly corruption in original sin, taught by Augustine, which reinforced the emphasis upon closing one's eyes to the external world. Spiritual illumination came through entrance into the "cloud of unknowing,"[9] or a movement from what Dionysius called "kataphatic theology," images and concepts about God, to "apophatic theology," the denial of images and concepts in favor of knowing without knowing (a direct perception of God in the "cloud" that transcends intellection).

This type of spirituality has dominated Western religion; the church has, in fact, often rejected and persecuted proponents of other types of spirituality. Because neoplatonic spirituality is based upon suspicion of all things natural and corporeal, asceticism becomes the mark of the spiritually elite. And any type of spirituality that *affirms* the corporeal and natural in humans and that is nonexclusive is to be rejected.

Mundane Spirituality

The second type of spirituality may be called "mundane" spirituality. This is the spirituality of the seventeenth-century Carmelite Nicholas Herman (Brother Lawrence) and the twentieth-century Protestant Frank Laubach. This kind of spirituality is not influenced by neoplatonism, does not view spirituality as the climbing of a ladder, and is not elitist. Rather, it begins by acknowledging the presence of God in human life, claims that its method is for all people, and relates spirituality to mundane circumstance. Its method is simply to carry on an internal conversation with the divine, who is one's companion throughout every occasion of life. It may be practiced while tending to things in the kitchen (Lawrence's circumstance) just as well as, if not better than, at the altar. All that is done and thought is directed to God. According to Brother Lawrence: "Our sanctification does not depend upon changing our works, but in doing for God's sake all these things which we commonly do for our own." Sin is acknowledged, but is given over to the Companion without ado. Brother Lawrence writes:

> When I fail in my duty I simply admit my faults, saying to God, "I shall never do otherwise if You leave me to myself. It is You who must stop my falling and it is You who must amend that which is amiss." After such praying I allow myself no further uneasiness about my faults.

What is the result of this spirituality? Lawrence describes being "lifted up" to the "very center and being of God." He exclaims, "I believe no more! I see!" So persistent becomes this "practice of the presence of God" that, for him, the "set times of prayer are not different from the other times of the day."[10]

This "ordinary" type of spirituality does not deprecate the natural and the human. It directs attention to and affirms divinity in the mundane. In that way it allows change of consciousness to be achieved gently through the work and promptings of the divine companion. It does not practice self-mortification. It makes its claims for all people and excludes none from the depths of the spiritual life.

Creation-Centered Spirituality

The third type of spirituality is the ancient creation-centered type discussed briefly in Chapter 2. What needs further description is its method.[11] Spiritual growth occurs in four stages. It begins with the positive way (*via positiva*), which involves the discovery and affirmation of the blessing that is already in creation. This path therefore sets forth the notion of faith as trust in the Creator and in the goodness of creation. In this stage, sin is acknowledged as the human decision to negate what the Creator blesses. The view of Christ becomes the affirmation of the creation in the Incarnation.

The second stage is the negative way (*via negativa*). The difference between this spirituality and the neoplatonic type known as purgation is that creation-centered spirituality replaces purgation with a process of "letting go" and a "befriending" of darkness. The process frees one from ideology and for receptivity to what may be found in darkness. Sin is the refusal to admit the need for receptivity and therefore the refusal to develop receptivity. The view of Christ employs the *kenotic* theme ("to empty out") found in the hymn to Christ in Philippians 2:1–11, wherein Christ empties himself in obedience to God.

The third stage is the way of creativity (*via creativa*), wherein a rush of creativity accompanies the befriending of our divinity. Sin is viewed as the volitional misuse of what is good, and at this stage we are to focus upon Jesus as poet, storyteller, and artist. The final stage is the way of transformation (*via transformativa*), wherein the devotee learns and affirms celebration, compassion, justice, and prophecy. Sin is the "cold heart" that leads to indifference to creation and Creator. Here Jesus is the agent of the new creation.

It is important to notice that creation-centered spirituality begins and ends with blessing and is blessing oriented throughout all the stages of spiritual growth. It acknowledges and takes seriously human sin, but at no point does it deny the goodness of what is natural in human beings and in experience. Thereby it leads to a profound transformation of the whole person and positively orients the person to nature, others, and God. It makes connections in all directions and at all levels by means of the intrinsic beatitude embedded in the cosmos and, thereby, in us.

Incorporating Spirituality into Life

It may be seen from this all-too-brief sketch of the three types of spirituality that the predominant neoplatonic type is essentially world and life denying at its base. It leads to a profound suspicion of all things natural. In contrast, the other types affirm the goodness of all things and view the natural world as gift and treasure. Moreover, only the neoplatonic type is elitist.

The Science of Discernment

I would maintain, therefore, that the neoplatonic type of spirituality does not help us gain the perspective required to develop an ethic relevant to the environmental crisis. Nevertheless, its representatives, such as Ignatius of Loyola, were concerned with ethics and explored what is called the "science of discernment."[12] For Ignatius, discerning the promptings of the Spirit of God leads to ethical action that is Christian. Discernment of such promptings, he thought, relies upon faith, investigation of our "dispositions," or feelings, and a mystical experience productive of joy, peace, and security in our actions. Those ethical actions that are not established in this manner produce inner turmoil. In addition, Ignatius would have us test the signs of the Spirit with norms of Scripture, reason, indifference (i.e., detachment from inordinate affections), and conscience. Contemplative theologians followed him in attempting to refine this science. Their goal was to adopt a life-style commensurate with the inner dynamics of spirituality. That is, they sought ways to follow the God met and known in mystical experience. We can thank them for the beginning they made.

According to contemplative theologian and historian William Johnston: "The art of discernment is still developing; and I believe it will be of cardinal importance in the decades which lie ahead. This is because, as I have said, complex and difficult decisions are arising in the lives of good people and a legalistic ethic is unable to cope with them."[13] Johnston calls for two explorations by those working in the field of spirituality that should help develop the science. The first involves a dialogue between spirituality and psychology, because psychology, especially of the Rogerian kind, will offer profound guidance in the understanding of human feelings. The second exploration must be dialogue between Buddhists and Christians, because Buddhism's long experience with what it calls "mindfulness" enables the devotee to gain an inner liberation ("indifference," for Ignatius) and, thereby, total awareness. Although I agree with Johnston's conclusions and with the intention of the science of discernment, I would point out that its contribution to ethics and a Christian life-style will be forthcoming only as it is liberated from the neoplatonic foundations that inform its spirituality generally. This means that discernment must be liberated from the anthropocentric, nature-denying worldview of neoplatonism. Here the creation-centered type of spirituality is of crucial importance.

Creation-centered spirituality is a comprehensive method for affirming nature, for liberating us from ideology, and for becoming receptive to the promptings of the Spirit. Further, it stimulates inventiveness and creativity regarding ethical life. Thus, reclaiming this type of spirituality will be of benefit to theology, Christian piety, and, most especially, to theological ethics. It can enrich the science of discernment as an ethical science for, above all else, it will renew our orientation to a God at work in the biosphere (panentheism), so that we come to see the biosphere as the treasure, blessing, and gift that it is. Here again, our way of thinking and our way of living could be changed.

Mysticism and the New Testament: Jesus as Model

I indicated at the beginning of this chapter that there are grounds for understanding Jesus in the light of mysticism, and noted that New Testament scholars are beginning to work from such a perspective. Although there is much work yet to be done, the investigation is important, because it begins to unearth the source of Jesus' own closeness to and understanding of God. It explains the source of his own powers, message, fearlessness, prophetic authority, self-understanding, and compassion. Indeed, everything about him is illumined in a new way when we see him in the light of Jewish and other forms of mysticism. That he could insist that he knew God, was one with God, bore the message of God, and knew God's will and intentions for the world suggests an immediacy of divine-human encounter that is known to the mystical traditions worldwide. As I shall demonstrate in the next chapter, his ethic is properly understood at its root from the perspectives of mysticism.

New Testament investigation on the basis of mysticism represents prospects for advances in Christian thinking and action. Consider the process:

1. Jesus *the man* received his power and authority, his message and knowledge of God, as a gift from God. In the thinking of all the world's mystical traditions, that is as it should be. "Enlightenment," the "Prayer of Union," or "divine-human

communion" are always a gift. One does not accomplish such things. They happen; they are given.

2. The gifts reveal the openness to reception of the gift of the one to whom they are given. That openness, or receptivity, is a human capability that, in the words of the creation-centered tradition, may be nurtured and refined through a process of "letting go."

3. These gifts bring union with God, joy, love, compassion, prophecy, justice making, wisdom, healing powers, fearlessness, gentleness, strength for nonviolent action, and a clarity about priorities and mission.

These characteristics, found throughout mystical literature, read like the New Testament's catalogue of the attributes of Jesus.

Was Jesus the man a mystic? Yes. Was he a man? Yes, and in the words of biblical scholar Albert Nolan, "a much underrated man"! He was a remarkable human—a "lord" among the mystics of the world, because in the brief span of not more than three years (the span of his ministry in John's Gospel), he left a clear mark of God upon human history that is unequaled. Was he "Emmanuel" (God with us) *as a man?* Yes. Jesus revealed God to humans because he gave what was given to him. He became an open channel for this gift giving. He gave these gifts with unequaled clarity, courage, and inventiveness. And the giving cost him his life, which God then gave back to him as the gift of resurrection.

Thus, as a man he was the firstborn of a new, human possibility—the possibility of a new God-filled humanity on earth. He saw it as his mission to create this new humanity by calling others to follow him and to assist them to receive what he had received, and thereby to follow him in the kind of self-giving life he lived. Jesus gave to humankind the prospect of a new way of life that is first and last a gift of God, and which has as its context his own spirituality of receptiveness, prophetic insight, and compassion.

What of us and our forms of spirituality? As Jesus was "a much underrated man," so too his view of us has been underrated. The dominating Western fall/redemption model of salvation and the enigmas of the ancient fourth- and fifth-century creeds about the nature of Jesus' person have created a sharp distinction between what he was and what we are or may become. With very few exceptions, the Christian churches have never entertained the prospect of humans actually being or becoming like Jesus *in all respects.* Yet the New Testament is replete with evidence of his call to others to follow him and become like him in all respects. Were this not so, then his injunctions and teachings ("You must be perfect, as your heavenly Father is perfect" [Matthew 5:48]) would constitute a self-conscious mockery of human potential.

The more usual Christian objection to my thesis is that we cannot be like Jesus because of our sin, and that therefore his call to follow him is not a mockery but a call to salvation. From the vantage point of mysticism, however, his call may be seen as a call to become like him in all respects, because it is a call for us to be the recipients of the same gifts he was given by God. In short, we are capable of achieving Jesus' kind of spirituality as humans, and as capable as he was of being anointed by the reign of God he proclaimed. We too could light and season the world with the heavenly unction given him. We too are capable of the divine gifts that were his stunning attributes. At all points he said to his fellows and to us, "Follow me!" Does that not mean: "come with me; live as I do; do what I do; attain my gifts, stature, attributes, and powers that come from the Father in heaven"? Yes, he is our savior, because he shows us the path to his own powers. There is no magical, supernatural person here. Rather, there is an enlightened, God-illumined mystic leading us to the God who transforms, enlightens, and empowers life now and into eternity. To follow such a one would mean trusting in his own high and ennobling view of human capability before God. It is a capability that, when filled with the gifts given him, could transform the world with love as did he.

Mystical Theology: An Example

Thus far we have been investigating mystical theology and its types in a rather abstract manner. A practical illustration will enable the imagination to perceive it. Imagine the following.

You are sitting with a group of people in a room that has a closed door. The door has no handle and can be opened only from the other side. I am with you in the room, and I am the mystic. That means I have a friend beyond the door. Occasionally, the friend opens the door to me and grants me audience. We build a relationship that is initiated and sustained by the friend. I gain trust in the friend thereby. The relationship and the trust I designate by the word *faith*. Often I think about the friend, about our relationship, and about what the friendship has done for me. Everything I do in the room has as its foundation the constant awareness of the door and the friend beyond. Often I retire alone to the door and speak through to my friend. Sometimes I am granted audience.

One day you ask me to tell the group in the room about my friend. To answer your request, I must think through our relationship in detail. In the process I must make of the friend an *object* for the mind to consider. This is quite inappropriate to our relationship, because all along I have known and lived with the friend as a *subject*. Nevertheless, I ponder and, using whatever skills of intellect I may have, I construct for the group a "doctrine" concerning my friend. I tell you, as best I can in language, what in the last analysis cannot be said. I point with words to the living reality of my friend, our relationship, and what I have become as the result. You ask me questions about my language. What do I mean by thus and so? I answer as best I am able.

Let us say that another person in the room is suddenly granted an audience with the friend. She returns to the room with the announcement, "Bowman is wrong about the friend!" Whereupon another doctrine is put forth to the group. I had said the friend was large. The new mystic announces that the friend happens to stand four feet tall! I respond that I meant large in the sense of being big hearted. "Then say 'big hearted'!" responds the new mystic. Notice that the two of us are engaged in a "doctrinal disputation" about the friend. We argue about how best to convey with words the living reality of the friend who, in the last analysis, is beyond words. In this case I lose the disputation and had best watch my language. Does losing the disputation alter or harm the living character of my relationship with my friend? Not at all.

Rather, I have been instructed as to language, and for this I should be thankful to the second mystic.

Some in the group may still favor my original presentation over the new doctrine. Hence a split occurs among believers in the room. Odd? That is how the church has split apart over the centuries on the issue of the creeds, their meaning and interpretation. Note how far removed doctrine is from faith. Yet, so long as there remains social conversation within the room about the friend beyond the door, doctrine is important and demands critical refinement for meaning of any kind to be forthcoming.

The next day someone in the room announces that she wishes to know the friend firsthand, and asks if the two mystics would help. The two of us point to the door and suggest a method whereby she may get to the door—not through it. Herein the types of spirituality are constructed. Each mystic articulates how each remembers getting to the door. One says, "I had to leave all of you behind, be made clean from the corruption in this room, and climb a ladder to the door. There I had to wait long years before the door was opened to me." The other says, "There are no ladders to the door. Rather, it all began with my sensing something like the 'presence' of the friend already in the room. It was a kind of premonition of the friend on this side as well as on the other side of the door. I simply followed the premonition around the room, where I found not corruption but blessing, and, to my astonishment, I found myself at the door 'befriending a solitude' that seemed nourishing. One day I too was granted audience, and, when given back to myself, I opened my eyes to see that the entire room was radiant with the beauty and love of the friend I had met! The friend opened my eyes to see the friend in everything, everywhere, loving, suffering with all things, nourishing all and granting to all inexpressible blessing. The room is not corrupt! It is the blessed handiwork of the good friend. It is a gift!"

Notice that both mystics made it through the door. Both were granted audience. The question I have explored here is not which method of spirituality best gets us through the door. The friend does that and may use in us any method. The question of importance is, Which method best articulates a view of the *room* that is commensurate with the character of the friend met and known? Is the room evil, corrupt, and awaiting destruction, or might we consider its "lilies of the field" the handiwork of a good friend deeply interested in the room's survival?

For three hundred years many in the churches have said there is no "door" or possible audience with the friend. Some long ago somehow gave us word from the friend. We must *believe in* their word. Yet, for three hundred years the "lilies of the field" have waved in a gentle wind, and we have not noticed them in a manner that could change our way of thinking.

FOR DISCUSSION

1. In what ways has this chapter helped you appreciate how people come to know God? Are there experiences of your own that parallel what has been suggested in the text?

2. What, according to this treatment, is the place and relevance of doctrinal discussion and disputation? How can it enrich spiritual life?

3. How can spirituality help change our way of thinking?

4. We all have favorite places. Close your eyes and go in your imagination to that place. Allow it to work its magic on you. Now return to where you are. Discuss the differences. What would it mean to live here out of the riches of that favorite place? How is this similar to mystical life here wherein God is the "favorite place"?

4

AN ETHIC TO TRANSCEND
MODERN LIMITATIONS

What is the nature of ethics and of all ethical reflection and action? Or, more basically, What does it mean to live according to the new way of thinking?

The answer to the question is by no means self-evident even for those trained in philosophical and religious ethics. Numerous ethical systems have been devised in the Western world. Some of them are religious systems; most are philosophical in their orientation. Some are a blend of philosophy and religion. Moreover, there are numerous Christian ethical systems. Which are relevant for the new way of thinking? Which are not? Given all of this, we should not be surprised to learn that most of us are uninformed about the formal ethical disciplines; in fact, a majority of Christians have no idea of what the field of theological ethics involves.

Thus, to answer the question in a Christian context, which is the aim of this book, we will first review the dynamics of all ethical reflection and action. Then we will move on to an analysis of the unique ethical guidance provided by the Scriptures. Finally, we will consider the relationship between the new way of thinking and Christian ethical action. This endeavor is crucial, because a new way of thinking that fails to result in relevant ethical life is worthless.

The Dynamics of Ethical Reflection

To understand the nature of ethical reflection and action requires an understanding of the vocabulary involved. Theologian Paul Lehmann has demonstrated that in ancient Greek and Roman philosophy, *morals* came to mean "behavior according to custom," whereas *ethics* came to mean "behavior according to reason."[1] Although the distinction no longer pertains and we use the terms *morals* and *ethics* interchangeably, the original distinction will help us understand what is involved in all ethical reflection and action, including Christian ethical reflection and action.

All societies, ancient and modern, have had clearly delineated customs. Following those customs meant being moral, according to the ancient Greek and Roman definition. Ethical reflection, on the other hand, came into existence when philosophers such as Socrates subjected custom to the criticism of reason in order to discover a better way of doing things. The question became, Is the moral way, that is, the way of custom, the best way? With that question philosophical ethics was born. Hence, ethical reflection had as its object morals or custom, critically evaluated for the betterment of human life. The critique employed reason as its tool; hence, the better way—that is, the ethical way—was the rational, or reasonable, way.

This process of analysis could and often did lead to the conclusion that to be ethical one had to go against custom. To be ethical could logically mean, therefore, being immoral. We can comprehend, then, the seriousness of the charge against Socrates by the Athenian court, which was "corrupting the morals of the youth of Athens." Socrates was convicted of the charge and sentenced to death, because on the basis of reason he advocated going against Athenian custom. Ethical reflection and action have often been dangerous endeavors, no matter what the culture or society.

There are other ways to subject custom to criticism. One can, for example, subject the customs of one culture to criticism based upon the customs of another culture. Colonialism has done this by imposing the morals of the captors on the captives. This illustrates a competition of morals but not true ethical reflection and action, according to the ancient Greek and Roman usage. It represents nothing more than a power struggle of morals, using a criticism based on prejudice, not reason. This social criticism can result in a transformation of custom, but not of any underlying patterns of thought or belief.

In addition, one can subject custom to a critique based upon a theological, or religious, perspective. That is, the critique of custom is made according to one's knowledge of God. The result will be a theological, or religious, ethic. It is here that this discussion may help us understand the dynamics of the Hebrew prophets and the teachings and ethic of Jesus—in fact, all theologically based ethical reflection. For that matter, it can help us understand the reaction to the teachings of the prophets and Jesus by their contemporaries. The prophets were advocating a radical change of custom based upon God's perspective. They were replacing custom with theological ethics, and as did Socrates, they paid the price of such dangerous enterprise. In the words of Mohandas Gandhi, one must be prepared for "mountains of suffering."

There are two important ingredients required for understanding ethical reflection. The first clearly is custom. The second is a theological, or religious, perspective that is brought to bear upon the custom in question. This is what Karl Barth meant when he insisted that Christians should think with the Bible in one hand and the newspaper in the other. The Scriptures provide the theological perspective, and the newspaper the clue to custom.

It may well be that when we put the two together we do not necessarily draw the conclusion that the ways of custom are wrong. Gandhi advocated the customs of his people on religious and practical grounds, but reflection led him to resist the British custom of empire. On the other hand, when we try to square theological perspective with societal custom, we may arrive at what Robert McAfee Brown has called a "confessional situation" in which we are forced to say yes to God and no to our local caesars.[2] Such was the situation of German Christians under Hitler. Ethical reflection on a theological basis forced them to reject completely Hitler's National Socialism. Today, Christians must reflect ethically upon the customs that have created the environmental crisis, and ask whether such a "confessional situation" has been reached. Will our analysis lead us to say yes to God and no to the caesars of government and industry?

Incorporating theology in ethical analysis or reflection, however, complicates the issue, for differences of perspective arise from different interpretations of the faith. This accounts for the many theologically based ethical systems advanced throughout Western history. Moreover, it further clarifies the controversies between the Old Testament prophets and their theologically oriented contemporaries, and Jesus and his theologically oriented contemporaries. Depending upon the theological interpretation, culture and custom are read differently, which causes controversy and leads to frustration. We do not have "a Christian ethic." We have Christians' ethics. The many different churches and denominations have different perspectives based upon their varying interpretations of the Scriptures and church traditions. Thus, the question arises, Who has the appropriate perspective from which to criticize custom in a cogent Christian manner and perspective?

Obviously, we are also in a position to understand how a way of thinking can complicate one's theological perspective and thereby influence theological ethics as well. Modern thinking can and does influence the interpretation of the faith. If one's cast of mind involves deterministic, mechanistic, anthropocentric presuppositions, the theological perspective that results will reflect those presuppositions. If one's reality is distorted by presuppositions, the accompanying theological perspective will itself be distorted, and the ethic that follows will be distorted. Accordingly, ethics can founder upon the shoals of consciousness. Therewith the deeper problem of ethical reflection and action is seen. How can we be certain our view of reality is correct? How can our theological perspective be freed from illusion and produce a critique of custom that is accurate and cogent? These questions deliver us over into the agony of ethical reflection and the subsequent making of ethical decisions.

To turn the problem around, consider that if postmodern thinking calls into question the canons of modern thinking, then a modern theological perspective, rooted in those canons, is itself questioned. Postmodern thinking calls for a new theological perspective and hence a new theological critique of modern custom. Postmodern thought provides a new understanding of reality, and with that a new perspective for ethical analysis.

The Ethic of Jesus

Where are we to look for guidance in such a frustrating, agonizing, and dangerous enterprise? The current ethical impasse may be rooted in an accompanying impasse of contending worldviews. How can we test which worldview is correct, adopt it, and move on to a constructive and accurate ethic? I believe that, because what we are after is a Christian theological perspective for our theological ethic, it would be helpful to examine now the ethical teachings of Jesus in order to understand the guidance given in the New Testament. Jesus' own world was one of contending theological perspectives and in its own way experienced an ethical impasse much like our own.

Matthew 5—7

Two passages from the New Testament are important for understanding Jesus' perspective. The first is from Matthew's Gospel; the other from the book of Mark. The Sermon on the Mount (Matthew 5—7) is an excellent starting point. Its beginning, as Matthew structures the sermon for us, has Jesus addressing his audience. The "blessings," or beatitudes, addressed to the audience may also be found in Luke's Gospel and, given their nature in Luke, should warn us against the tendency of so many to "spiritualize" these blessings in Matthew. That is, Jesus' audience represents society's poor and needy, not the religious and political leaders, and certainly not those who live comfortably in some interior spiritual world. They are the poor, whom Jesus calls "blessed" and adds that they are already the "salt" and "light" of the world. Jesus tells them that he intends to uphold Jewish law, but to do so in such manner as to lead them to a righteousness that exceeds that of their religious teachers. His clue to them as to the goal of their ethical analysis and activity is contained in the statement "Your light must shine before people, so that they will see the good things you do and praise your Father in heaven" (Matt. 5:16, TEV). The goal is to give glory to God and not to glorify, justify, or otherwise call attention to the self. How is that done?

In Jesus' one ethical teaching that scholars agree is not already found in the Hebrew Scriptures, namely, to love the enemy, he adds that such action is taken for the sake of being like God.[3] The point is to emulate God. In this way one calls attention not to self, but to God. Thus, one must gain God's own perspective if one is to emulate the Father in heaven. Being already "blessed," already "salt" and "light," Jesus' followers are to act in such a way as to demonstrate God to the world through that saltiness, light, and blessed nature. The intention is not to call attention to self or justify the self as righteous. Ethical analysis and action is done to demonstrate God to the world. To do so, one must have God's perspective and understand the divine way, the divine custom. This, of course, was Jesus' own intention and life's mission—the demonstration of God before the world.

The other injunctions in Matthew are troublesome. They are taken from Jewish law, but Jesus seems to make them into internal, terrible strictures. You have heard you shall not kill; I say anger is equivalent. You have heard you are not to commit adultery; I say the lustful look is equivalent. Who can escape such devastating indictments? None can, and that seems to be the point. The burdens these injunctions place upon Jesus' hearers are worse than those of their religious teachers, whom they are now to exceed in a higher righteousness. Furthermore, Jesus seems to mean what he is saying, because he concludes with the injunction "You must be perfect—just as your Father in heaven is perfect" (Matt. 5:48, TEV). Who can be serious about such a radical ethic?

Mark 10:17–27

We gain insight into these difficult injunctions by examining another instructive passage found in Mark 10:17–27. There the rich man kneels before Jesus and asks the question burning in the minds of his contemporaries, "Good Teacher, what must I do to inherit eternal life?" Jesus stops him there and asks his own question, "Why do you call me good?" Then he reminds the inquirer of the primary canon of Jewish thought, "No one is good but God alone." God alone is good, holy (*qadosh*), righteous (*sedeq*). It follows from this that we must see that God's action alone is to be considered ethical action. God's perspective alone leads to the better way, the higher righteousness. Jesus is therefore suggesting that the first commandments of the Hebrew decalogue (Ten Commandments) indicate the primacy of God in all things, including ethics, and therefore, implicit is the question, Have you God's perspective and knowledge of God's ethical activity? It would also follow from this that human action is ethical only insofar as it participates in or is commensurate with God's action. "No one is good but God alone" rules out independent human action entirely.

But the rich man wants to discuss "doing" for the sake of salvation. Therefore Jesus moves to the last section of the decalogue and recounts those injunctions. These the man had followed from his youth. His conscience was clear, and he may be considered a "good man." We are told that Jesus loved this good man. Thus, it must have been because of love that Jesus enjoined him to sell all that he had and follow him.

As the man retreated downcast, Jesus reflects aloud about the difficulties of "doing" for the sake of salvation. Such manner of entrance into eternal life is difficult, especially for the wealthy. In point of fact, all of Jesus' ethical teachings make prospects for entrance into eternal life extremely difficult. Although we may not kill, who can avoid anger? Ethical action for the sake of salvation *is* difficult. Thus, the disciples ask of Jesus the appropriate question toward which the entire passage before us moves, "Then who can be saved?" Jesus answers, "With men it is impossible, but not with God; for all things are possible with God." What are we to make of this?

If we understand the dynamics of this passage and the Sermon on the Mount, we must conclude that the goal of ethical action is not salvation. Salvation is the gift of God, for whom all things are possible. "Fear not little flock," said Jesus. "It is your Father's good pleasure to give you the kingdom" (Luke 12:32). Our future is in the hands of inexpressible love. Ethics has nothing to do, therefore, with earning such an unmerited gift and must focus somewhere else completely. The focus and intention of ethics are to gain the perspective of God to the end that we might participate

Very good distinction but not one "taught" too often.

Studies in Moral Development

in the divine way and act in such manner that others come to praise God or acknowledge that "God alone is good." Earning salvation is irrelevant and unconnected with ethics.

To return to the difficult injunctions found in Matthew 5, we can understand that Jesus places the burden upon his hearers not to make them try harder to earn salvation. No. Rather, his injunctions drive home the message that our perspective is not God's perspective. Therefore we cannot hope to emulate the Creator when our perspectives lead us to actions that contradict God's way. We hate and kill; God loves and gives life. We steal; God is generous in blessing beyond imagination. We betray with all forms of adultery; God is faithful and stays with all people through thick and thin. We lust and seek conquest; God blesses and gives freedom. In all ways our actions contradict God's way, according to Jesus, because we know neither God's perspective nor God's way of doing things. The real question of ethics becomes, therefore, What is God's way and perspective? Humans need to turn around and catch the vision of the divine way. Otherwise, God's way, which alone is good, seems ludicrous and impossible to us, and we continue our destructive pattern. Earning salvation through ethical action is not the point. Rather, ethics follows from our knowledge of God and from the fact that we know ourselves to be already blessed and loved by God.

The Ethic of Paul

The same point is made by Paul in his letter to the church at Rome (Rom. 12:1–2). Benjamin Reist has called these two verses Paul's "preface to ethics," for they provide insight into the ground, ingredients, and goal of a Christian ethic. The ground is knowledge of the "mercies of God" upon which the whole perspective for a Christian ethic is based. This ground is the same ground for all of Jesus' ethical teachings.

The first ingredient for ethical action is our flesh-and-blood existence, our body, which Paul insists is "spiritual." That is, there is no dualism in Paul between spiritual life and the natural life of the body. When we put our bodies on the line for the sake of ethical action, we are engaging in spiritual worship. What else can

offer your bodies as a living sacrifice, holy & acceptable to God — your spiritual worship. DO NOT CONFORM yourselves to this age but be transformed by the renewal of your mind so that you may judge what is God's will, what is good,

be spiritual existence, if not our natural existence as embodied creatures? The second ingredient for an ethic is our enlightened perspective, that is, our renewed mind. Ethical action is intelligent action, else it becomes sentimental and irrelevant. Christians should have no quarrel with philosophers and scientists who enjoin us to use our heads.

Thus, with a perspective founded upon knowledge of God's mercy and with concrete and intelligent action, we are to do what? Earn salvation? Not at all, according to Paul. His answer (v. 2) is complicated by a rich Greek verb *dokimadzein*. Although translated "prove" in most English Bibles, no single English equivalent is to be found. The verb means literally "to put to the test so as to approve and pronounce worthy." What are we to put to the test so as to approve and pronounce worthy in our ethical action? We are to acknowledge God's will and way as worthy of being pronounced good, acceptable, and perfect. Attention does not focus upon us or upon salvation, but upon God's will, goodness, acceptability, and perfection. In short, ethics means testing and demonstrating the goodness of God before the world. This we are to do concretely in our embodied existence and with enlightened intelligence.

If this understanding of these New Testament passages in question is correct, we should be alerted to the need for discovering God's own perspective, for we humans are to adopt God's own way of thinking. That is the foundation upon which Christian ethical critique of custom is to be based; it is action calculated and accomplished for the sake of emulating and illustrating the worldview of God before the world. Thus, the question of ethics becomes the question already explored in the previous chapter, How can we know God and God's way directly? The answer is spirituality, the gift that God alone gives. Spirituality is the ground of ethics, as it is the ground of all Jesus' attributes and powers. We are invited by him into this new possibility that is within human capacity spiritually and ethically.

pleasing & perfect

Postmodern Thought and Its Implications
for Ethical Action

This understanding of the Christian ethic should enable us "to put to the test so as to approve and pronounce worthy" the habits of mind that are called modern and postmodern.

What we are about to consider is relatively new in Christian circles. The more usual tests for doctrine, ideas, discourse, and ethics have been tests of reason and logical coherence, the adherence to creeds, tradition, or particular biblical interpretation, and the like. Here we reverse the process in the sense that thinking is subjected to the test of ethical relevance. In short, thinking and doctrine that fail to provide constructive ethical guidance are to be held suspect.

I am convinced that the limitations inherent in modern thought (see Chapter 1) rip apart the holistic fabric of perceived reality and lead to denial and destructive tendencies founded upon a static, dull, mechanical view of life. In every respect they contradict what Christians know to be the ways of God as found in the Scriptures. To accept that the modern way simply represents the inevitable propensities of human sin and that, therefore, we should bow to the inevitable and hope for future grace carries the determinism of the modern worldview into Christian thinking with a vengeance! It leads Christians to repeat the question "Are we to continue in sin that grace may abound? By no means!" thunders Paul in Romans 6:1–2. We have been called to "newness of life" (6:4) by the mercy of God. We can and must turn around and adopt habits of mind commensurate with the biblical message, else we extract the ethical nerve from Christian faith and baptize, through our indifference and lack of a renewed intelligence, the dull and deadly customs of modern society. Many Christians are doing just that. They are calling people to salvation while at the same time sanctifying the political, economic, and agricultural policies that reflect the destructive attributes of modern thought. They have uncritically adopted the modern worldview and with skin-deep thinking have fostered the fabrications that lead to the denial of God's earth. With that, Christian salt becomes tasteless, and the light goes out.

Such could hardly be called the demonstration of God's goodness before the world!

The postmodern vision, although still in formulation, seems to fit best the biblical view of a creation grounded and sustained in the mercies and love of God. The vision replaces separation with connection, competition with cooperation, destruction with blessing, and denial with vibrant affirmation. It replaces determinism's lack of ethical sensitivity with ethical perspective, responsibility, and sensitivity. It positively relates us to the biosphere and, because it acknowledges how we are connected to all creation at the subatomic level, lifts before us the "preferential referent of nature." With that, it radically challenges current policies and action that ignore nature as being the good handiwork of a good God. It drives home Jesus' own critique of the human perspective that ignores the relationship between the Creator and the lilies of the field. It moves in scientific, philosophical, artistic, and social directions that Christians can support. It makes for a new Song of Solomon concerning the earth and its blessings. It adds the grace note we all seek in life.

An Ethical Posture: The Example of Dietrich Bonhoeffer

All sorts of ethical systems have been constructed in the West. Some are theological systems; most are philosophical. What is important is that most of them are *systems*. By that I mean that they tend to be contained and closed. Their creators put a period at the end of the system and say, "That's it." In so doing they attempt to capture and encompass all reality within the system. As we have seen, however, the postmodern vision views reality as open, dynamic, changing, evolutionary. Accordingly, the construction of a closed system is ruled out. Reality will itself explode the confines of the system and remove the period at the end of the sentence. Upon reviewing the processive character of reality, Benjamin Reist concludes that "*perspectives* are far more important on such a path than *systems* ever can be."[4] The thought of constructing an ethical system these days is no longer possible or desirable. What we should seek in ethics is a posture and a sensitivity founded upon perspective. A posture indicates a way of approaching reality and life. It suggests a style—directions and guidelines, not rules—and is open-ended intrinsically. Sensitivity suggests moving beyond rules and laws to a creative engagement with the spirit of the perspective.

At this point I want to introduce the thinking of Dietrich Bonhoeffer. He was a German Lutheran theologian who died a martyr in a Nazi prison during the closing days of World War II. His last writings from prison have prompted considerable theological discussion during our century, and it is clear from those writings that he wished to contribute to the formulation of a Christian ethic appropriate to the late twentieth century. His work is incomplete but, nevertheless, has been sufficient to prompt new ethical perspective for scholars. I draw upon his thinking here because I believe it can illumine for us the relation between the New Testament ethic I have just explored and the issues of the environmental crisis we all face. His thinking provides tactical guidance for translating the biblical ethic into a postmodern world.

It is with an understanding of perspective, posture, and sensitivity that we can best understand the relevance of Dietrich Bonhoeffer's ethical reflection. He was not interested in constructing a system, because the starting point he chose was his own recognition of the dynamic complexity of reality itself. He moved from writing his *Habilitationschrift*, called *Act and Being*,[5] that acknowledged the static, closed character of systems, to concentrate upon the dynamics of Reality (*Wirklichkeit*). In 1932 he wrote: "What the sacrament is for the proclamation of the gospel, the knowledge of Reality is for the proclamation of the commandment. Reality is the sacrament of the commandment."[6] By this he meant that ethical reflection must be founded upon a concrete knowledge of reality. An ethic that does not find its root in reality is irrelevant and lacks concreteness. Likewise, an ethic founded upon a distortion of reality is itself a distortion. Reality itself becomes the test and norm for an adequate ethic.

As Bonhoeffer's reflections move from this beginning to the development of his *Ethics* and *Letters and Papers from Prison*, the ethical question and the issue of tactics for ethical action radically changed from the systems and reflections of the past. The new question became how best to perceive the depths of a reality that includes "God and the cosmos,"[7] or what Paul Lehmann, following Bonhoeffer's lead, calls discovering "what God is doing in the world."[8] The tactic for ethical action becomes how best to speak and act out the living truth of reality in such manner as to illumine that reality, or better, to illumine a reality that includes "God and the cosmos." What is at stake is an ethic relevant to the nature of reality itself, an ethic that does not lie "somewhere out beyond reality in the realm of ideas."[9]

Bonhoeffer wrote a brief critique of ethical systems that do not follow his criteria for reality.[10] He compared systems of reason, principle, conscience, duty, freedom, and private virtue against the dynamic complexity of reality, and demonstrated how all fail and fall victim to distortion when "reality lays itself bare." All produce in the end the image of Don Quixote doing battle against a foe and for a lady that do not exist. What is telling in each failed system is the lack of reference to God and to nature, or, according to his understanding, to the totality of reality. Bonhoeffer's critiques are cogent, but, because he was under the dominance of the anthropocentric modern paradigm, they are not as convincing as they could have been. What I stress here, however, is the relevance of his *method*, in which the totality of a reality that includes God and the cosmos is the touchstone, the norm for ethical reflection and criticism.

Following Bonhoeffer, it becomes clear why modern thinking with its anthropocentric orientation fails to provide ethical or conceptual resources for coping with the environmental crisis. Modern humanity feels kinship neither with God nor with creation. Both are unknown and unfelt. Both have no preferential place in the formulation of modern strategies for directing human affairs. Anthropocentrism rules supreme. Moreover, because the anthropocentric system is enclosed within the mental notion of a rigidly fixed machine, ethical systems remain fixed and machinelike. They do not allow for novelty, dynamism, or the open-ended emergence of a universe that is alive and evolving. In the end, reality is denied conceptually and ethically. Indeed, current political, economic, industrial, social, and agricultural policies founded upon modern thinking are themselves idealistic in their assumption that somehow the continuation of current policies will bring us through the period of the inexorable destruction of the biosphere. But in fact it must be recognized that these policies and the way of thinking they are founded upon are bankrupt.

The biblical message we have explored and the reflections of Bonhoeffer comparable to that message enable Christians "to put to the test so as to approve and pronounce worthy" the postmodern vision and way of thinking. Both test modern thought and pronounce it unworthy.

Tactics for Ethical Action

The lesson to be carried from Bonhoeffer into the formulation of a postmodern, Christian ethical posture is that an ethical act must be instructive. It must point up a reality that includes God, nature, and humans.

Those who have studied Bonhoeffer's work have concluded that his ethical posture may be called "contextual" ethics. The point is important because it is suggestive of the tactics to be employed in behaving ethically. We have from Bonhoeffer the fragment of an essay entitled "What Does It Mean to Tell the Truth?"[11] In it he gives a simple illustration:

> A teacher asks a child in front of the class whether it is true that his father comes home drunk. It is true, but the child denies it. . . . The teacher's question has placed him in a situation for which he is not prepared. . . . What goes on in the family is not for the ears of the class in school. . . . The child's answer can indeed be called a lie. . . . Yet, to the measure of his knowledge the child acted correctly. The blame for the lie falls back entirely upon the teacher.

Bonhoeffer concludes that telling the truth is an art that must be learned, because telling the truth is the attempt to put what is real into words. The child did not realize that what was real at that moment was that the teacher's question failed to acknowledge the boundary existing between the contexts of family and school. The teacher overran the boundary and therefore masked it from the view of the child and class. In the last analysis, by distorting the context in which it was asked, the question produced the lie. Had the child more experience, he could have unmasked the masked boundary and revealed the true context in which the question was being asked. The child could have said words indicating, "Teacher, this is none of your business, nor is this the place for such a question."

Being ethical and telling the truth are equivalent; both must be learned. Telling the truth means finding the right word that illumines the moment for all concerned. So too, the ethical act is that right action that instructs as to what actually is the case in any given context. To be ethical, then, we are to move from moment to moment, or better, from context to context, and learn to be sensitive to the total reality of each context in order to illumine each context. This does not mean that we move without benefit of guidance drawn from previous experience; rather, we bring with us into each new context the resources experience provides for guidance. We do not build an ethical system; rather, we build ethical sensitivity through experience. In the words of Jesus, we become wise as serpents while remaining harmless as doves.

One of the failings in the more popular working out of the contextual ethic known as "situation ethics" is the view that we move from situation to situation *de novo,* without benefit of guidance, and approach each new situation as a novice. This thinking fails to comprehend the depth of Bonhoeffer's contextual approach. We do have resources as we move into new ethical situations. Those resources may include family background, education, and religious training. They produce, along with our experience, the perspectives that guide tactics. I recall discussing with a student a dilemma she faced. We were exploring the possible options for action she had available to her. I asked her to tell me which option she would choose. She mentioned it. "Why that one?" I asked. "Because that is how my folks would act," she answered. The context of family informed her reading of the present context and indicated a tactic. So it is with Bonhoeffer's approach, and he insists that we continue building that resource for guidance through education and experience drawn from responsive engagement in life. The process of learning must never end. Never should we stop and say, "Now I have my knowledge, theology, and ethic settled and complete." That would mean a return to the closed irrelevance of a system.

Bonhoeffer's approach to a Christian ethic is similar to the approach of Jesus and Paul in that all three call for the demonstration of God in the world. To Bonhoeffer, this means the demonstration of a total, contextual reality that includes God. His critique of ethical systems that are removed from reality and that are the "realm of ideas" is especially cogent. His articulation of contextual tactics that drive toward concrete instruction about reality is helpful and contributes to our practical understanding of the teachings of Jesus and Paul. But he fails to explain how one comes to know the reality that includes God, thereby leaving unexplored the issue of spirituality as the ground of ethics. But an appreciation of spirituality completes our understanding of his ethic as well as the ethic of Jesus and Paul.

A Model for Reflection and Action

In the light of these discussions, I now propose a model of the process of ethical analysis that leads to ethical strategy. The controlling question is, How might one determine the strategy for action? The question is crucial, for it concerns the *means* of ethics. I would offer the following steps:

1. The first step is a commitment to responsibility. The ethically sensitive person does not retreat from life into indifference. This means, therefore, that one takes learning seriously as a lifelong commitment. Keeping current about world affairs, for instance, is as important as reading about ethics. Only then can the concrete relevance of what we are reading be tested and intelligently employed.

2. The ethical situation arises. This usually means that current events challenge or even threaten our posture and worldview. Something demands reaction. No longer is the question *whether* we should act, but *how* we should act. To be sure, there are times when events call for such immediate action that we have little or no time to reflect. We act instinctively. Nevertheless, in such moments our instincts are most likely dependent upon the depth

of our previous ethical reflection and action. It is such reflection and preparation when we do have time for reflection and calculation that I outline here. How well and how consistently we do that will be of great benefit in occasions requiring immediate action.

3. We engage in a theological analysis of the context. Are we informed? Bonhoeffer observed that "knowledge of an apparently trivial detail quite often makes it possible to see into the depth of things." He points out that such perceptiveness distinguishes mere knowledge from wisdom, and that wisdom is grounded in our capacity to be without prejudice. I take this to mean that one is without ideology and is, thereby, open to receive reality and learn from it. Moreover, Bonhoeffer adds that such openness is a mark of the health of our theology. In his own words, we are free from prejudice when we "belong simply and solely to God."[12]

Paul Tillich frequently remarked upon a principle of perception found first among the Old Testament prophets. Cryptically put, the principle says that one does not relativize the absolute or absolutize the relative. For the prophets, the absolute is God alone. All else is relative, including human thought, institutions, and governments. To absolutize the relative means making a god out of what is relative—elevating human institutions and thinking to a position of divine prominence, which is idolatry. To relativize the absolute means not taking God alone with ultimate seriousness and, thereby, mixing God's mystery and wonder with human things and models. All of this illustrates what Bonhoeffer intended in his method for acquiring wisdom for an ethical analysis of the context. A healthy theology recognizes the relativity of all human enterprise before God, and that recognition frees us from prejudice and our own propensity for ideology. God alone is taken seriously with awe and reverence. All else is relative and may be subjected to critical scrutiny—from religious and philosophical creeds to our own pet ideas. With such freedom we are to investigate the context.

4. Several strategies may be suggested by the context itself. These we must place alongside custom, experience, and the worldview that we bring to the context. All go into the mix of our analysis, and we begin asking questions: Is custom correct? Are

the options that are indicated by the context itself altered by the perspectives and experience we bring to the context? Does our knowledge of God suggest better options? Above all, which tactic illumines best the character of the total context we perceive?

5. We act according to our analysis and our best option, keeping in mind that instruction and the illumination of reality are our goals. We are not earning points for heaven. We are engaged in education about the context, which above all else includes the fact that God alone is good. To overlook that fact is to miss completely the meaning and purpose of our reflection and action.

6. We observe what happens as the result of our action. This is crucial if we are to learn anything of ethical and tactical relevance for the future. Examining the results of our action allows us to continue to build the experience beneficial for future living. People, especially students, often retreat from ethical activity because in their own judgment their first attempt failed. Thus, they walk away from life and learn nothing for the future. Moreover, they do not understand that failure can be instructive and is most likely the richest resource for continuing education. Consider Paul's "preface to ethics" in his letter to the Romans (Rom. 12:1–2). His thesis was that we are to demonstrate the goodness of God to the world. What if we fail? The ethic is based upon the "mercies of God," has nothing to do with earning salvation, and, therefore, is free for failure. We may pick ourselves up before the merciful God, examine how and where we went wrong, and re-engage the world in a new attempt that is better informed and more experienced. Christian ethical systems that build upon the notion of ethics as related to salvation, that see ethical action as earning points for heaven, cope with human failure by instilling guilt and fear into the one who fails. How can we square that approach with a biblical message called gospel, "good news"? What is good news about a theology and ethic that makes humans ashamed and guilty in the face of failure? Does not such an approach blunt the edge of resolution and misdirect the focus of true ethical education?

Finally, most often we do well to reflect and act in conjunction with others. There are times when we must act alone. But to act alone out of volition and mere preference is dangerous. There is a collective wisdom in humankind that is at most superior to our own individual wisdom, and we are well advised to acknowledge that.

Gandhi: A Model for Action

The model for ethical analysis and action is best understood through illustration. Among the many available, I would choose to have Christians ponder the methods and tactics of Mohandas Gandhi of India.[13] Martin Luther King, Jr., took pains to study Gandhi's methods and tactics with care, and employed them fruitfully as a Christian. In that sense he drew upon the wisdom of humankind that transcends Christian faith, an important and far-reaching possibility we must come to appreciate.

Gandhi was thoroughly Hindu and Indian, yet his education was English. He understood the British people, and, above all, he valued them. He knew deeply the British sense of honor and fair play that permeates their customs. Accordingly, he did not consider the British people enemies. In fact, he did not view any person as enemy, an outlook informed most especially by his Hindu theology and ethic. His true enemy was colonialism and the policies it spawned that destroyed the Indian people and their homeland and contradicted the best that was in British culture and tradition. The sword of colonialism cut both ways, destroying captors along with captives. The symbol of true colonialism was found in a Latin inscription that appeared on the buckles of British military belts during the period of the British *raj*. Translated, the inscription read, "For Sake of British Trade." There is no more illuminating depiction of what colonialism of any form means, namely, power employed for sake of wealth.

Gandhi knew that if he could instruct the British as to the destructiveness of colonialism for both Britain and India, their better nature would respond. They would turn from their destruction of India and possibly free it in such manner that it could join the Commonwealth as friend and ally. The resulting Indian freedom would be good for the lives of the Indian people and good for the soul of Britain. Hence his question was, "How can I instruct the British of the evil of their ways while keeping them as friends, not enemies?" This was the primary tactical question behind his actions and his life, and is comparable to the "serpent and dove" concept enjoined by Jesus of Nazareth.

Not so incidentally, Gandhi was a man of profound spirituality, as well as a student of the New Testament and other world scriptures. Although a Hindu, he was profoundly ecumenical and could say that he was at one and the same time a Hindu, Christian, Jew, and Muslim. My father took me to a railroad station to hear Gandhi speak, although I was very young and do not remember. He told me, however, that, to his astonishment, Gandi read to the Indian people the Sermon on the Mount, enjoined his people to live that way, and with that closed his address, returned to the train, and rode off. Because his perspective was deeply religious, his ethical tactics were religiously based. That meant, for him, non-violence was the only valid methodology and option. Never would he harm another. Never would he humiliate, dishonor, or harm the British people. Rather, he sought ways to instruct them.

Because Gandhi's chosen strategies were nonviolent, he and his people had to be prepared to endure "mountains of suffering" at the hands of the unenlightened among the British government and military. He was certain that "mountains of suffering" would eventually set the stage for the British to take notice of the situation in India. Thus, his tactics sought to heighten consciousness concerning colonialism itself.

Eventually, the British press came to India in force, making possible their instruction. The famous "salt march to the sea" was the instructive occasion beyond all others. The press was there. Gandhi reached the sea, took up a chunk of salt from the sand and declared it "Indian." He was arrested and imprisoned. Why? The press published the answer. British salt trade in India forbade the Indian people to collect and process the salt from their own country. They had to purchase it from the British and pay a salt tax. Soon after this symbolic act, India was free.

The symbolic act was Gandhi's genius. A good example may be found in Gandhi's audience in London with the King for the purpose of discussing the Indian problem. Gandhi had chosen to wear the simple dhoti of the Indian peasant, "an indecent rag-of-a-thing," according to one Londoner. After the meeting, Gandhi was greeted with the question, "How can you dress like that before the King?" He answered, "Did you see the King? I thought he was dressed grandly enough for the two of us!" The press and the people got the message: India was in rags so Britain could go in royal dress.

Gandhi's analysis of the situation of his people under British colonialism was spiritually based, intelligent, and critical. His tactics were contextual and sought to be instructive. The whole of reality was thereby illumined. Christians can still learn from him, as they can learn from Jesus. Both men articulated in words and deeds what a spiritually grounded ethic could mean. Both assumed an inventive "posture" guided by "sensitivity" to reality. Therefore, both were able to illumine for us a vision of reality that leaves nothing out. Indeed, both contributed to the betterment of the world they knew, because they followed to the very end a way of thinking that was different—a way of thinking that reflected God's own perspectives. And they did it with undaunted courage and with style.

Practical Implications of a Postmodern Way of Thinking

In this chapter I have delineated a contextual, theological ethical posture that is derived from the New Testament and the thought of Dietrich Bonhoeffer. I have attempted to show that such a posture is commensurate with the new postmodern way of thinking. A model for ethical analysis and action has been sketched, and an example has been provided.

But what relevance has this approach for Christian living and action in a time of environmental crisis? What concrete guidance does the treatment suggest? There are six practical implications of my proposal: education, awareness, creative simplicity, global perspective, consideration of the long-term consequences of our decisions, and the power of personal example.[14]

Education

The first and possibly most important guideline derives from the emphasis given to the demonstration of a reality that includes

God, humans, and nature, or what has been described as the educational task of the ethical act. This means that the place to begin is with education—education of one's self and others about the realities of our time and the prospects of a postmodern Christian perpective that will illumine these realities. In other words, what the world desperately needs is information and heightened consciousness, the awareness of the fact that the global, environmental crisis is the primary and most crucial issue the world currently faces. That crisis should constitute the primary agenda item for all our institutions—from the churches to government. Indeed, it may be argued that the current pathology of all our institutions—including the churches—is evidenced in their refusal, for a variety of reasons, to make the environmental issue their principal agenda item.

Awareness

The psychotherapist Frederick Perls developed his analytic and therapeutic methodology known as "Gestalt therapy" around the axiom that awareness is itself therapeutic. His aim was to enable his patients to break through their neurotic avoidance of obvious reality and their confusion about their obvious and immediate reality into "awareness." This would mean that the patients would break out of the impotence produced by their avoidance and confusion and, through the light of awareness, would have creative energy and capacities for coping with reality. His successful practice provided evidence for the wisdom of his method as well as for the truth of his axiom.

Perls' Gestalt therapy provides psychological verification for the first guideline I have drawn from the theological ethical posture advanced in this chapter. Heightened consciousness through education means awareness, and awareness is therapeutic because it breaks through avoidance and impotence to clarity, potency, and creativity. Awareness makes possible a change in thinking and action because it elicits our creative potential.

On these grounds, I would argue that the greatest service the churches could render the world at this time is providing education concerning the facts of the environmental crisis, the ingredients in our current thinking and action that contribute to the crisis, and the resources we already have available to us for altering our way of thinking and action in constructive ways. In many instances this may mean that Christians may have to become unpopular and frustrating irritants in a society characterized by avoidance. They may have to join forces with environmental groups that are a thorn in the side of many of our political, economic, educational, and yes, religious institutions. They may do this in order to push our society to break through to awareness. Because, as we have seen, such an educational enterprise is at the heart of the ethical enterprise enjoined by the Scriptures, it follows that to avoid awareness of the earth's present environmental condition is to avoid, in our time, the meaning of the message of Jesus. What else, after all, is implicit in the prayers "Thy kingdom come, Thy will be done on earth as it is in heaven," if not the desire to have accomplished on this fragile globe, which we are systematically destroying, the will of a God we know loves the creation? To acknowledge the love while ignoring the destruction is to deny the prayer.

Creative Simplicity

Specific practical guidelines may be drawn that cut across the grain of our infatuations with materialism, individualism, and anthropocentrism. For example, the once popular "Shakertown Pledge" called for a life of "creative simplicity"—the intention "to reduce the frills and luxuries in our present life-style but at the same time to emphasize the beauty and joy of living."[15] All Americans can choose this, with the exception of the poor who have no other option. Our wealth and waste are obvious when measured by the fact that the average American man, woman, and child uses twenty-two tons of the world's mineral resources per year. Consider the elements, fuels, products, and forms of energy that make possible our rich life-style during the average day, and ponder the fact that we remain, nevertheless, a people characterized by stress, overweight, discontent, and physical or mental dis-ease. Simple living means the reduction of both waste and the exploitation of the world's resources.

The postmodern way of thinking and the theological ethic commensurate with it call for living in a creatively simple manner when applied to the context of environmental devastation. There is no alternative.

Global Perspective

The Shakertown Pledge indicates yet another guideline implicit in what I have argued. It begins by suggesting that we all declare ourselves to be world citizens. This does not mean that we fail to love our country, home, and hearth. Rather, it means that we acknowledge primarily that we are citizens of a global community that extends beyond the village pump. Moreover, it means that we acknowledge that our human lives are all connected to a vast, global network of life, human and nonhuman, that is interdependent.

Concretely, such a declaration and such acknowledgments lead to the further acknowledgment that the real marks of what we call success are not competition and possession, but cooperation and contribution. The image of that wondrous picture of our earth taken from the moon comes to mind. How do we study that photograph and deny that we are all citizens of one earth?

Long-term Consequences of Our Decisions

This discussion suggests a question that should always remain in the back of our minds as we make our decisions: What are the long-term and global effects of my decisions and actions, seen over against the more usual short-term and limited decisions made in the rush of modern existence? This question is as relevant to a social ethic as it is to a personal one.

Power of Personal Example

The final guideline rests upon the assumption that humans do have power, in spite of our fantasies of impotence derived from fear. This means that human example and action can be potent and meaningful. Dietrich Bonhoeffer wrote: "The church must not underestimate the importance of human example (which has its origin in the humanity of Jesus and is so important in Paul's teaching); it is not abstract argument, but example, that gives its word emphasis and power."[16] Here, I believe, is the real clue to how we move a theological ethic from the realm of abstraction, theory, and perspective into the concrete arena of flesh-and-blood existence. We must recognize that our actions—our decisions, words, and deeds—can influence other lives and can alter the course of history. Ponder the power of and the effects produced by one, tired black woman who refused to move to the back of a segregated bus. That action launched a national movement. Ponder the power and effects produced by one Irish housewife who, upon witnessing the killing of a British soldier outside her door, called a personal halt to hatred, confronted her neighbors with the alternatives of peace and compassion, and went on to become a Nobel Peace Laureate whose common and simple touch caught the attention of world leaders. Our refusals, our responsible and compassionate actions, our individual styles and gestures, our words, anger, tears, and humor can have enormous potency and impact. And need it be mentioned that Jesus' ethic rests upon just such a high view of human potential?

These guidelines do not exhaust the enormous potential of the ethical posture advocated in the Scriptures. As a place to begin, however, it seems certain that education, awareness, creative simplicity, global perspective, consideration of the long-term consequences of our decisions, and the power of personal example are all concrete ways we may demonstrate the goodness of the God who gives to us life in such an inexpressibly beautiful world. What is more, each guideline, if inventively and courageously enacted, could restore the Christian hope that the accomplishments of heaven be manifest on earth.

E
A
C
G
L
P

FOR DISCUSSION

1. What customs (moral ways) in our society contradict or distort the reality of life as Christians perceive it?

2. What is the goal of the Christian ethical act according to this chapter? In what ways is it liberating? In what ways is it difficult to consider and pursue?

3. What kinds of issues do you consider genuine ethical issues for Christians today? Review them in the light of the model for action set forth in the chapter.

4. In what ways could Christians relate to the tactics of Gandhi? In what ways were his actions instructive as to a context that includes the fact of the goodness of God? In what ways were Jesus' actions similar?

5. In what ways might the churches demonstrate the goodness of God to the world? How might such action contradict or challenge the customs of our society?

6. In what ways does the postmodern vision of reality relate to the teachings and ethic of Jesus?

7. What, according to this treatment, would constitute an unethical act?

5

MEDITATIONS ON A
NEW BEGINNING

There Is Hope!

What a time to be alive! Humankind has dawning upon its consciousness a new perception of its origins—the nature of life, the world, the universe, God. We have seen our world's beauty from afar. We have begun to appreciate its deep connections, its ecology. We may know as never before of our alliance with one another and with all things on earth and in the heavens. Unlike our forebears, we may begin to glimpse the image of a dynamic, interactive, wondrous creation that causes us to say the words *God, beatitude, cosmos, nature, life,* and *humankind* with new meaning. We stand on the threshold of a new time for the earth, for we are confronted with the prospect of taking a new evolutionary step. We are challenged to enter into a new life by the prospect of adopting a new way of thinking.

Although our generation is at the threshold, it must be acknowledged that some have been here before us. Too often they have been the reviled and scorned women and men of cultures and generations too fearful or too blind to understand them. They transcend their times and their cultures. Some have been revered or worshiped—after they have been put to death. They have been here and have given us news of their discoveries. They have described the goodness of this new prospect, this new way for humans. They have spoken its words of joy, hope, promise, liberation, healing, justice, peace, love, compassion, spirituality, and faith. They have told us of the loving Creator who has brought us to this threshold. They have shown with deeds the new life possible. With passion they have warned us of the old gods we must leave behind if we are to embark upon the new path. They are the gods of mammon, ideology, prejudice, and hatred—gods worshiped by a wrong way of thinking.

We stand where they left off. No longer dare we overrun their thinking with our modes of thought. No longer dare we scale down their message to fit the cultures and institutions of the old gods. No longer can we remain complacent before the truth of their vision, which we are being forced by events to see. No longer dare we elevate them to such heights of sainthood or divinity that we fail to know them as fellow humans and take their words seriously.

They have warned us where we are headed if our way of thinking and living persists. We are headed for nuclear and environmental disaster—perhaps both at once—that would be unspeakably grim. Without argument, we are headed for environmental catastrophe at a rate that means there is no time to waste; change must begin now. Thus, we must value their vision, which reveals, at one and the same time, the limitations of our thought and the possibility of alternative new/old directions.

We have explored types of spirituality in the Christian West—in particular creation-centered spirituality that, because of its comprehensiveness and direct relevance to the ethical perception of reality and the discernment of the will of God, is to be favored. An ethic has been delineated so as to demonstrate the relevance for life of the worldview we are challenged to adopt. The guidance of the Scriptures, when combined with the insights of Bonhoeffer and Gandhi, makes for a posture that reorients us to the ethical question and the issue of tactics. In short, we have been shown how to live out the new meaning in the words *God, beatitude, love, compassion, faith,* and *justice.*

Although the new worldview has yet to take hold and be understood critically and thoroughly, we must advocate it, because it does relate deeply to the best that is or could be in humankind. It is not an external imposition upon us of some new doctrine. Its seeds, inner truth, are already in us and in all creation about us. What we must do is cultivate that inner truth.

To be sure, if history teaches lessons, it certainly teaches that the modern way of thinking is not likely to vanish overnight. In some respects it should not, for aspects of it make possible important advances of science and logical thought. Nevertheless, given the dangers of the modern world and the limitations of the modern worldview, we should speed up the process of change to the new vision in those areas that relate us in new ways to one another and to nature. The biosphere will not tolerate our indifference and our brutal tinkering with its dynamics, balance, and fragile fabric for much longer. Moreover, there is hope embedded in this vision, a nonsentimental hope founded upon the critical and realistic understanding of the dynamic universe that sustains us. The vision can do what Einstein, Reist, Sittler, and a host of others call for. It can change our way of thinking before it is too late for thought of any kind.

Beware Our Caesars

The threshold upon which we stand requires us to ask whether we have reached what Robert McAfee Brown calls a "confessional situation" regarding the environmental crisis.[1] A confessional situation means that we have been confronted by a clear breach of the First Commandment: "You shall have no other gods before me." In other words, we would have encountered a human institution elevated to the place of divinity. In Tillich's terms, the relative would have been absolutized. The result would be an idolatry that says, "Forsake your god, for Caesar is now god." We would have confronted a context that, in Bonhoeffer's thinking, obscures the nature of true reality. No longer would it be a question of *whether* we should respond, but of *how*. The tactical question would confront us with urgency, and we would have to begin the process of analysis and questioning outlined in Chapter 4, recognizing all the while that instruction should be our aim and that we must act.

Brown himself believes that we "may be moving toward a *status confessionis* in two areas: nuclear weapons and the national security state."[2] He has documented how administrations attempt to become impervious to the voice of the electorate. The National

Security Agency, for example, is not directly answerable to the electorate. We do not elect its membership. This means that there is a government within the government that does not directly account for itself to us. Accountability is indirect and may be circumvented. Brown writes:

> A good example of such logic is the 1983 piece of White House-initiated legislation mandating that all public officials who have access to classified materials and who want to comment on public affairs, either now or in the future, must obtain governmental clearance for their remarks ahead of time. The provision applies not only while they are in office but *for the rest of their lives.* This provides a powerful weapon to those in public office to forestall knowledgeable criticism by those best informed to provide the service.[3]

Thousands of public officials have already agreed to abide by this unrescinded piece of legislation.

A government that is unanswerable to the electorate is not only undemocratic, but is also close to demanding an allegiance commanded by the First Commandment of the Decalogue. We begin to hear, "Caesar is your God. Trust him to do what he knows is best for you!"

At this juncture it is imperative that we learn from history. John Dillenberger and Claude Welch demonstrate how, contrary to the other reformers, Martin Luther failed to work out the implications of his doctrine of God for the state.[4] For Luther the state had a negative function; its function was to constrain chaos and keep order. This is why he attacked the Peasant Revolution of 1524. On the other hand, his loyalty to God meant an unmistakable stand against tyranny. However, he did not relate the state's negative mandate to the Christian's ultimate allegiance to God.

Adolf Hitler brought order to a chaotic Germany. He fulfilled, in his own terrible way, Luther's mandate to the German nation. The tragic experience of Christians in Germany was that they responded too late. Not until the cross had been removed from the altar and replaced by the swastika did they awaken to the fact that Hitler had gone too far and had breached the biblical commandment. By then Germany was locked into the mind-set of its new caesar.

If, as Brown thinks, we are moving toward a confessional situation in this country, our task must be to prevent it from developing. We are not to wait, allow it to happen, and then respond. We must seek nonviolent means to insist that the entire government be answerable to the public. Moreover, because we live in a nation wherein there is an irrefutable link between government, the military, and industry, these institutions must be made answerable to the people through the workings of democracy.

I once was in a car with someone who could be called an "industrial prince." He delivered an hour's diatribe on the evils of governmental restrictions on his company, evils fostered by what he called "ecology freaks." He was considering moving his plant to another country where restrictions are fewer. It became clear from his statements that radical individualism informed his economic theory and his orientation to the world. After all, his was but one company forced to compete with the "giants," the multinational corporations that span the globe with a power and wealth exceeding the controls and wealth of most nations. He and his company had to survive alone, and the restrictions fostered by the "ecology freaks" were destroying his chances of survival. The destructions of pollution caused by his company were a drop in the bucket compared with the destructions caused by the "giants." Let the world cope with them and not with him and his miniscule operation!

"One must start somewhere," I countered. "Perhaps your firm could set an example and start a new trend?" His response cannot be put in print. This made me ponder what might be the response of corporate giants to my suggestion. It is clear enough that any company or nation that sees itself engaged in a struggle of competitive survival in a world of individualism and noncooperation will share his outlook. None will begin a new trend, for all gauge their wealth and health by the standards of capital and profit. None will pause to consider that wealth and health are *not* measured by capital and profit. The real wealth in the world is the living richness of the biosphere itself. The world's health is the health of the biosphere. None can breathe capital; none can drink profit. The creatures of the earth must breathe clean air and drink pure water. In our competitive rush for capital and profit we have forgotten what constitutes the real wealth of life that exists apart from all the capital and profit known to the industrial institutions. Our governing economic theories have obscured from view the true wealth of nature and have perpetrated an illusion. Capital and profit are the ingredients that feed the god mammon. That god is demanding that we sacrifice the wealth of nature as our appropriate spiritual worship. One day, very soon, all we will have left will be our capital and profit, and the god mammon will be satiate with our folly.

My car companion also let slip that his wife spends in one month's shopping what I make in a year. My salary is three hundred times the individual income in Nepal. I thought again of the inscription on the belts of the British military during the days of Gandhi ("For Sake of British Trade," power employed for the sake of wealth). I asked myself, Is this why the governmental/ military/industrial complex in this nation seeks to remain unanswerable to the electorate and possible criticism? If that be so, we must acknowledge that America is becoming locked into the mindset of all empires. If that be so, let us beware of its caesars. They may bring evolution to a halt.

Anawim—Today's Oppressed

There is another side to consider. In George C. Wolfe's stunning play *The Colored Museum*, a character appears onstage looking about at the world and exclaims, "If this is the answer, then we've been asking the wrong questions!" The line is an indictment, not of God, nor for that matter of the natural world, but of human culture. It is street prophecy. The character is black—a gay black man of the city. He is an outcast, and he knows it. He speaks for the outcasts of the world, for the *anawim* of the Hebrew Scriptures, the oppressed of the earth, the most numerous of the human species. He has no credentials other than the essential credential of the *anawim* who must struggle for survival among the "haves" and the "have nots."

He has no history other than pain and luck. He has no family other than the wretched of the earth. His root is the street where, with his own salt and light, he must season and enlighten his own becoming. His salt has become a sharp savor too caustic and brackish for the stews of gentility. The light in his eye flashes the white heat of suffering and hostility. His gaze can sear his audience, which he puts on the defensive.

He is a "son of man" who must find a place to lay his head each night. For him, fasting is no fad. For him, cunning has become a virtue. The reality of poverty creates his conceptual frame, his philosophy. The belly aligns priorities and makes clear the distinction between wants and needs. To live through another day unscathed is entertainment. Laughter is luxury. Adversity is tutor. His economic theory is derived from the principles of the hunt.

His politics? He and his kind have lived under every political system designed by humans. They have tested every political system and found all unresponsive to wretchedness. Should he ever have occasion for redress, the request would be for what we call "justice." But the word would likely sound like "revenge" when he sounded it in the halls of any established order that has kept him controlled, impoverished, and unseen. He knows he has no occasion for redress. He has no advocate other than himself. So he asks only for "luck in the hunt" and casts his prophecy to the winds with a wry humor.

Because he is and remains unseen, he and his kind enjoy a unique freedom. He is free to be what he is, to establish his own fashion and style. He is free for his own judgments and assessment of the human condition. He is free for his own inclinations. His life is his own secret.

Has he an ecological sense? Likely he doesn't even know the word. But he could teach us of the waste, squalor, pollution, and destruction of modern urban society. These realities are his environment. Amidst them all he must forge life. His senses are alert to the smells, tastes, and feel of toxics. He matured early to these realities. He will die early if he does not continue to learn and be on guard.

Wolfe has given the man's life articulation with one devastating statement. The statement does not praise him; it just reveals him. He can be as brutal and treacherous, as selfish and hateful as any.

After all, he is a "son of man" and no more. Were he to gain power, his corruptions could compound the human mix. He could turn away from the lowly as easily as any other. He could join the games of wealth and power unmoved by remembrance of what he once was. He never had time for blessing, compassion, and justice while surviving in a modern world that demands survival. Why should he change? How could he?

The question is, Does he know how common he is? Has anyone ever told him of the scope and dimensions of his kind? Does he know he is in the majority? Yes, and does he know that, despite the fact that the powers of the world give him no preferential place, the biblical word honors him? How? *His* kind were Jesus' associates and friends. To his kind the message was addressed. His kind were called "salt," "light," and "blessed." They were the "little flock" to whom it is the Father's good pleasure to give the reign of heaven. They were the ones healed, fed, forgiven, liberated, loved, and suffered for. Does he know that for his kind, God reserved the answer to the proper questions in life? Does he know he has an ultimate and compassionate "Advocate"?

More sadly, does he know that the good message of his Advocate became an institution that has often sanctified and blessed the powers that keep him impoverished and on the hunt? Does he know that many of those who create his squalor and filthy environment for the sake of their own gain and ease consider the Advocate their own? Does he know of the warnings sounded by the Advocate against such comfortable and uncharitable ingrates who worship other gods? Will anyone ever tell him of such "good news" in the name of God, his Advocate, and in the name of his fellow "Son of man" from Nazareth—tell him not with words alone but with deeds of liberation and healing?

Will anyone ever tell him it would cost seventeen billion dollars to feed, clothe, house, educate, and provide health care for every human on earth for one year? He could not conceive of such a sum. But does he know that *that* is what the nations of the world spend on weapons in two weeks? Does he comprehend the cost of keeping him in his place and the wealth of nations intact?

The powers of the world choose mammon every time. At the

very least, the communist countries are honest in saying they have not chosen God. Would that all the powerful were as honest! We could then acknowledge where a new beginning must be made.

An Ecumenical Agenda

In this book I have investigated areas of interest to Christians. But scholars have discovered remarkable similarities of resource in other world religions for the new vision. This is seen especially in what I have called the "mystical component" found in all world faiths. Reclaiming this component within Christianity can lead Christians to a deep ecumenism that transcends Christianity's dialogue with itself and moves to an enriching exchange among the world religions. Such enrichment is currently on the scholarly scene.[5]

Guiding Christians in this exchange is Paul's statement in Romans 8 that it is the "whole creation that groans and travails" awaiting adoption, and Romans 11, which suggests that all peoples are God's children. We are now beginning to understand that the wisdom of humankind, the individual and collective wisdom of people, can and often does transcend the wisdom of Christianity. We can learn much from one another. Gandhi's ethical wisdom is but one example. Now this does not mean that we should abandon Christian faith and seek a common, eclectic, new religious construct. It does mean, however, that we should draw deeply from our own well while paying attention to the wells of other faiths. Matthew Fox has shown that the creation-centered spirituality of Christianity acknowledges that God is the underground river from which all spiritual wells are filled.[6] If that be so, then the *Logos* of God (one could call it "the heart of God") that spoke through the man Jesus and revealed the glory, wonder, and mystery of the Creator is implicit in all wells sunk to draw on the underground river. We should look for its manifestation and affirm it in other faiths, not to deny religious identity, but for the sake of an instructive, interactive, and enriching religious pluralism.

The Next Step

What then could be our next step as Christians?

Theologians spend their working time reading, thinking, teach-

ing, and writing about theological matters. The public is unaware
of how close theologians sometimes walk to the edge of heresy in
their thinking. That, often, is how they explore, advance, and
learn. To be sure, they have norms, methods, and standards of
thought that govern their reflection and formulations. But very
often they push to the edge to see what might be there. Essentially,
therefore, they are explorers of the faith, scouts out on the fore-
front of knowledge. That is their vocation, and we should not
condemn scouts for having gone to see what might be. We should
hear their report and give thanks for their having returned alive!
Perhaps they will lead us into the new land of faith that is abundant
with milk and honey. Abraham is their model. He is the one who
followed God into the far country. I say all of this as preface to
what is to follow.

In January 1982, a colleague and I were a half day's trek out of
Tangboche monastery in Nepal on our way to Everest when we
came upon three Sherpa women with their yaks. One was a
secondary school teacher who spoke fluent English. "Please buy
something," she insisted, "I've had a hard day." Everyone in
Nepal wants to sell something, it would seem. It is a very poor
land by some standards, very rich by others. I bought a small silver
cup. With that our conversation turned to the usual introductions
and banter. Then I asked her in all seriousness, "Do you think you
can become a Buddha as a woman?" "Of course!" she responded
laughing. "But not in this life. I'm too busy." Then she asked me,
"And you, Christian Lama, will you become a Christ?" The question was to me *Vajrayana*, a "diamond-edged" thunderbolt. I don't
remember what I responded, but the remainder of the trek became
a searching meditation. Become a Christ? How unthinkable for
Christians! Blasphemy! And yet her question haunted me.

As I walked on, my mind became filled with recollections. Jesus
had insisted that his followers would accomplish greater things
than he himself. He had prayed to the Father that his people "may
all be one; even as thou, Father, art in me, and I in thee, that they
also may be in us" (John 17:21). Paul wrote of being "in Christ," of
"having the mind of Christ," of Christ "speaking through" him,
of "putting on Christ." In his letter to the Romans, he depicted

Jesus as being the "first" of a new generation of beings upon the earth. That night I fell asleep brooding over Paul's statement "I have been crucified with Christ; it is no longer I who live, but Christ who lives in me" (Gal. 2:20).

The next day, at 15,000 feet in the Kumbu Himel, I considered the proposition of Athanasius: "Christ was made man that we might be made God." At 16,000 feet, I thought of Luther's doctrine of the priesthood of all believers and its injunction that we are to become "little Christs" to one another. Another thunderbolt! "Become a Christ? Nonsense," I kept reminding myself. "It must be the altitude getting to me. Christians have never taken seriously, to my knowledge, the possible implications of these notions from Scripture and theological formulation. These are all figurative expressions, metaphors, and analogical statements—expressing likeness but pointing beyond themselves to qualitative difference.

Then at sea level, years later, at the Santa Barbara conference on a postmodern world, I listened to Matthew Fox discuss Meister Eckhart, Hildegard of Bingen, and the other Rhineland theologians. Their principal thesis was discover, affirm, and celebrate the "divinity in us." Thunderbolt at sea level! Moreover, conversations at the conference considered seriously the next evolutionary advance of humankind.

Recently I decided to think through the Sherpani's question once again. I was determined to remain calm, reasonable, and unmoved by propositions that would lead to utopian fabrication, even blasphemy. After all, Christology is about Christ, not us. We remain, in the Reformer's phrase, *simul iustus et peccator*. That is, so long as we live this life we are at one and the same time sinful and righteous—sinful, because of our nature, and righteous, because of the work of Christ and the Holy Spirit in us. This is the case as long as we live this life, that is. It may be different in heaven. So leave that to heaven! I read what Cyril of Alexandria had written following the Nicene controversy: "We are sons of God not by nature but by grace." Christ alone is Son of God by nature. We are not. There you have it. The distinction is technical, lucid, and means what it says. Become a Christ? Take heart Christians, nothing so radical is demanded of us.

Poor Sherpa women! They have to take seriously the prospect of becoming their Lord!

As I recalled the theological debate about how God's grace transforms us into children of God, Roger von Oech's "What-if game" engaged my attention. He has written a curious little book about thinking called *A Whack on the Side of the Head*,[7] wherein we are enjoined to ask ourselves "what if" regarding anything whatsoever, and ponder the ridiculous as answer. This is calculated to unclog the mind and free it for creative thinking. With that, I asked myself, "What if we became Christs?"

Obviously, the old encapsulated and brutal self in us would vanish forever. In its place would emerge our new natures in direct relationship with our Creator, who once provided the model in the man Jesus of Nazareth. Consider Jesus. He is the firstborn of this new generation of beings upon the earth, these "Christs." As long as he lived he was without home and possessions. It was his custom to retire alone to the hills for communion with God. It was his custom to give of himself totally to life with others with a power he himself said came not from himself but from his God, whose heavenly reign permeated every facet of his being. Thus, his whole life's act moved from that divine center and between the dual foci of solitude and life with others. The past he gave over to God. The future he left in the hands of God, and it was in the present that he lived for God and the world. He lived as though he had no family, for all who walked with him before God were viewed as family. His subordinates (disciples) he made his companions and friends. In all his associations he was open, forthright, and ultimately gentle and loving, with a powerful gentleness and love his followers were led to equate with the majestic love and gentleness of God. The two great commandments of the Hebrew Scriptures (to love God and neighbor) were his rubrics. Indeed, he became an open channel that brought God to humanity, a lens through which humankind could glimpse the mystery and wonder of God. This one, this man called the Christ the New Testament proclaims as the first of a new generation of beings upon the earth. As such, he brings judgment upon the old, brutal self in us and is the source of the new beings we are to become. His defeat and death bring to an end the rewards and expectations our old selves concoct for life. His mighty resurrection is the seal God places upon the life and destiny to be granted upon all, a destiny that all are to begin experiencing in this life. That is the good news the Christ reveals.

Become a Christ? That is what it would mean, and more: We would become the ones who could do no harm, for our wills would have fallen captive to the will of God, who sends rain on the just and the unjust alike. We would not seek ways to divide but to unite all manner of life on earth. We would be the poor, rich now with God's reign. We would be the mourners for the world who find comfort in God alone. We would be the meek to whom is given back the earth. We would be those who hunger and thirst for God's righteousness, which we freely give to all because we have been filled. We would be merciful with the mercy given us. We would be those cleansed of heart who see God. We would be peacemakers of the new generation of God's children. We would be those persecuted for sake of God's reign. We would be the reviled, whose joy overcomes the torments of a deadly and brutal world because God's joy is ours. We would be the little ones who light and season the earth with an unction given from on high. Our perfection would exceed all bounds, and we would know the "higher righteousness" of heaven. Human institutions could not contain the boundless reach of God's love that is in us. We would rupture the walls of religion with love!

And we would be prophets. What a wonder! We would see to the depths of things, because the greatest of depths has already freed us from all ideology. Therefore we would unmask and lay bare the evil in the world with nonviolent stratagems that refuse to engage the world in controversy on its terms. Our tactics would be at the ground level of love. We would cure the systemic cancers of corruption and oppression, and pay any price necessary to achieve justice, which for us would be the social synonym of love. We would reverence the handiwork of the Creator and, through noncooperation, shut down the destructions fostered by nations and institutions indifferent to polluting the earth and killing all of life.

This we would be and do knowing no shame, for our old selves would have known shame and death at the hands of Mercy itself. We would affirm the divine ray in all things. We would "consider the lilies of the field." That is, we would notice them, and we would laugh at the pomp and circumstance of the phony Solomon that once was in us, that used to seek glory and power and things—endless things—before we became Christs.

What if we did become all of these things? What if we could become Christs? Said Jesus concerning all of these things, "Ask and it will be given you." What if we did?

Appendix

THE NEW TESTAMENT'S USE OF THE "MYSTIC COPULA"

It was noted in Chapter 3 that the mysticism, or spirituality, of Jesus is being investigated by some New Testament scholars, a study that is given splendid treatment in Marcus Borg's *Jesus: A New Vision*. In this brief appendix I will attempt one modest contribution to that most important ongoing study and discussion.

As far as I am able to determine, recent scholarship has failed to consider fully the implications for an understanding of Jesus' mysticism found in those sayings attributed to him in the New Testament that reflect what historian of mysticism F. C. Happhold discusses as the "mystic copula."[1] Happhold writes:

> Perhaps it will help the reader to understand better if a word is said about what is called the *mystic copula*. When one makes a statement such as "This boy is John," one is using the copula "is" to express identity as identity is understood logically. When, however, Sankara says that the Atman is Brahman or Al-Hallaj said "I am Truth," neither are [sic] making logical statements of identity. In both the copula has a significance which it does not contain in logic. Both are mystical not logical statements of identity. Mysticism has its logic, but it is, to use Rudolf Otto's word, a "wonder logic."

Happhold goes on to document and discuss statements that reflect the mystic copula in sources drawn from a number of religious traditions. In describing the mystical union with reference to God, Allah, Brahman, or Buddha, mystics worldwide use statements that clearly reflect the logic of the mystic copula and tend to employ the verb *to be* within the context of such logic. Thus, when talking about the mystical encounter or union, a mystic will say such astonishing things as, "I am the All-Living" (the Sufi, Baba Kuhi or Shiraz) or "I am the One Real" (Abu Hamid al-Ghazali). Christian mystics have often employed the analogy of marriage or the union of lover and beloved in describing the Prayer of Union wherein the lover and beloved become one. As early as the Patristic period, Christian mystics have spoken of the union in terms of the "deification" of the human mystic in the encounter with God. As Happhold makes clear, such statements are not logical statements in the normal sense. Rather, they possess the "wonder logic" of mysticism.

Statements that the New Testament authors attribute to Jesus may also be viewed as representative of the mystic copula and its strange logic. The most notable, of course, are sayings in the concluding chapters of John's Gospel that suggest Jesus' intimacy with God (cf. John 14:8–11, 23; 17:20–22). Although these statements cannot be attributed to Jesus himself, they do reflect an early understanding of Jesus' relationship to God, in terms of the strange logic of the mystic copula, that became influential in the Christian communities. It is, of course, the task of the biblical scholar to determine what produced such an understanding in the early Christian communities. The questions I consider here are: What is this "wonder logic"? What does it indicate about the mystic's sense of identity with the divine? Could an appreciation of such a logic equip us to understand the meaning of the statements that incorporate such logic in the New Testament?

Happhold cites John of the Cross as follows:

> Then the two natures are so united, what is divine so communicated to what is human, that, *without undergoing any essential change each seems to be God*—yet not perfectly so in this life, though still in a manner which can neither be described nor conceived. (99)

He cites Henry Suso as follows:

> He forgets himself, he is no longer conscious of his selfhood; he disappears and loses himself in God, and becomes one spirit with Him, as a drop of water which is drowned in a great quantity of wine. (99)

And, finally, there is Teresa of Avila as follows:

Let us now come to the soul's inward sensations in this condition. These should be spoken of by those who know them; for as they are beyond understanding, so are they beyond description. I was wondering when I decided to write this—after taking Communion and experiencing that state of prayer of which I am writing—how the soul is occupied at that time. Then the Lord said to me: "It dissolves utterly, my daughter, to rest more and more in Me. It is no longer itself that lives; It is I." As it cannot comprehend what it understands, it understands by not understanding. (353–54)

What are we to make of these statements? Happhold and Thomas Merton provide the insight we are after concerning this strange logic.[2] Both authors make clear that what the mystic is attempting to express by the strange use of the mystic copula is that in the union being described the more usual subject-object mode of knowing breaks down and disappears. God is known as *subject* intuitively and immediately. God is not known as an object, and the *knowing subject* (the separate identity of the mystic) vanishes from consciousness and perception. One participates in the divine subjectivity without consciousness of separation as a knowing subject. For the moment, *all* is God. Then, as one is given back to one's self, a clear sense of separation from God and a clear sense of personal identity are reclaimed. In short, the logic of the mystic copula is the logic of intuitive encounter at a level that transcends normal consciousness. In attempting to convey the character of awareness during such an experience, which resists logical discourse and description, the mystic employs the copula.

What conclusions can be drawn from this understanding of the logic of the mystic copula? First, it is clear that the encounter and mode of perception being indicated are open possibilities for any conscious, knowing subject. Jesus, most certainly, could have had the kind of mystical relationship to God indicated by the copula. He could have intended his followers to emulate him by seeking a similar relationship that would be drawn, of course, from their close attention to his life and teachings.

Second, the identity being expressed does not denote an ontological identity. Jesus could use the copula without meaning, thereby, that he is ontologically God, that his being is God's being. He could use the copula to indicate the character of his experience and the source of his knowledge and power. Mystics have always done this. Thus, in this sense New Testament authors could have employed the copula when writing of Jesus—even have put such words in his mouth—in keeping with the Jewish tradition of monotheism and without violating either their monotheism or Jesus' identity as a human being. Moreover, it could fall to later generations of Christians, with different cultural and philosophical backgrounds, to draw ontological inferences of being and substance from such statements and sayings, inferences irreconcilable with the earliest traditions of Jesus' followers. Unfortunately, in the process the mystical character and power of Jesus' life, message, and worldview would be misunderstood, if not lost entirely.

NOTES

PREFACE

1. Throughout this treatment I shall refer to the "reign of God" and the "reign of heaven" as the appropriate translations of the more usual "kingdom of God" and "kingdom of heaven." The translation is in keeping with the findings of biblical scholarship concerning the Greek and Hebrew usage, avoids the popular misunderstanding of the terms as denoting a place over which a king has dominion, and leads to an understanding of the terms as denoting the quality of the God who reigns over the creation and human experience. See the instructive article on the subject by Joel Marcus, "Entering into the Kingly Power of God," *The Journal of Biblical Literature* 107, no. 4 (December 1988): 663–75.

2. Michio Kaku and Jennifer Trainer, *Beyond Einstein: The Cosmic Quest for the Theory of the Universe* (New York: Bantam Books, 1987), 115, 154.

INTRODUCTION

1. Cited in Matthew Fox, *Original Blessing: A Primer in Creation Spirituality* (Santa Fe: Bear & Co., 1983), 13. Fox rightly links the nuclear threat to the more inclusive ecological crisis in this remarkable book. It is imperative that we understand that all of the issues facing the world are conjoined in global scale. Moreover, as this book argues, all issues reflect the logical working out of the root dynamics of modern consciousness or way of thinking. Hence, the issues must be engaged at the root of consciousness itself.

2. Benjamin Reist, "New Theological Horizons in the Light of Post-Modern Science," *Pacific Theological Review*, Vol. 2, (Spring 1985): 4.

3. Details concerning population increase and land depletion may be

obtained from Werner Fornos, The Population Institute, 110 Maryland Avenue NE, Washington, D.C. 20002.

4. NASA's Robert Watson, chair of the Ozone Trends Panel, indicated that our use of chorofluorocarbons (CFCs) as refrigerants and solvents in electronics is depleting the ozone layer at a rate as great as 1 percent per year. A 1 percent decrease in ozone may be accompanied by a 5 to 6 percent increase in skin cancers (*Los Angeles Times*, 16 March 1988). The added ultraviolet radiation from the sun that penetrates the atmosphere not only harms human skin, but can, if present trends continue, burn crops and kill the oxygen-producing plankton in the sea. One more decade of unabated worldwide use of CFCs will bring on inevitable catastrophe. For a more detailed account of recent developments as to this serious issue, see John Gribbin, *The Hole in the Sky: Man's Threat to the Ozone Layer* (New York: Bantam Books, 1988). Gribbin adds to the Watson report, as covered in the *Los Angeles Times*, data concerning the contribution of nitrate fertilizers and the flight of supersonic aircraft, such as the Concorde, to ozone depletion. Although two international conferences have been called on this subject and much constructive work has been done and proposed, it remains to be seen whether governments and industries really appreciate its importance and urgency and are prepared to take profound, immediate actions appropriate to its importance and urgency.

5. Peter C. Hodgson and Robert H. King, *Christian Theology: An Introduction to Its Traditions and Tasks* (Philadelphia: Fortress Press, 1985), 2.

6. Henry Frankfort et al., *Before Philosophy: The Intellectual Adventure of Ancient Man* (Harmondsworth, Eng.: Penguin Books, 1951).

7. Ninian Smart, *Worldviews: Crosscultural Explorations of Human Beliefs* (New York: Charles Scribner's Sons, 1983), 1–2.

8. Einstein, Reist, and Sittler are not alone in their contentions. See also Philip N. Joranson and Ken Butigen, *Cry of the Environment: Rebuilding the Christian Creation Tradition* (Santa Fe: Bear & Co., 1984), 4–5. Sean Mc-Donagh, *To Care for the Earth* (Santa Fe: Bear & Co., 1986), pt. 2; Lewis Mumford, *The Pentagon of Power: The Myth of the Machine* (New York: Harcourt Brace Jovanovich, 1970), 413. It may be argued that the first to call for such a radical change and expansion of perspective in the modern world was Pierre Teilhard de Chardin. On December 22, 1918, he wrote: "I am more convinced than ever that our generation understands Christianity in a way that is too extrinsic and too individualistic. Dogma, both as preached from the pulpit and as it enters into the consciousness of those who receive it: (1) is something up in the air, above the universe, and with no connexion with it; (2) it seems to impinge upon only an *insignificant part* of cosmic reality. To present the Christian God as in a way external to and (even quantitatively) less than, nature, is in itself, to impoverish his being." See *Prayer of the Universe* (New York: Harper & Row, 1965), 17.

Teilhard then proceeds to the construction of a Christian cosmogony as a synthesis of love for God bound to love for the world. Teilhard scholar Conrad Bonifazi observes that Teilhard's originality was in constructing such a synthesis by binding Christ "to an evolutive world" as its personal center. In short, Teilhard held that Christ was related to the world "not accidentally, but organically and structurally, so that creation and incarnation were not two independent aspects of reality," but one the logical culmination of the other. See Bonifazi in Joranson and Butigen, *Cry of the Environment*, 316. In many ways the theological and intellectual revolution demanded of our times, which I attempt to elucidate in this book, may be seen as affirmation from many points of view of the cosmological vision sensed first by Teilhard.

CHAPTER 1. THE STRUCTURE AND LIMITATIONS
OF MODERN THOUGHT

1. See the helpful treatment of Descartes in Samuel E. Stumpf, *Socrates to Sarte* (New York: McGraw-Hill, 1982).

2. Fox, *Original Blessing*.

3. Matthew Fox, *A Spirituality Named* Compassion *and the Healing of the Global Village: Humpty Dumpty and Us* (Minneapolis: Winston Press, 1979), chap. 8.

4. Augustine, *City of God*, trans. M. Dods (New York: The Modern Library, 1950), bks. 15–18.

5. Dietrich Bonhoeffer, *Ethics*, ed. E. Bethge (New York: Macmillan Co., 1955), 196–206.

6. John A. T. Robinson, *Honest to God* (Philadelphia: Westminster Press, 1963), 65–67. Robinson concludes by saying: "But my point is not to say how far particular expressions, or the general trend of thought they present, verge on the limits of orthodoxy, but to put the question whether the entire supernaturalist frame of reference does not make anything but a Christological *tour de force* impossible. For as long as God and man are thought of as two 'beings,' each with distinct natures, one from 'the other side' and one from 'this side,' then it is impossible to create out of them more than a God-Man, a divine visitant from 'out there' who chooses in every respect to live with the natives. This supernaturalist view of the incarnation can never really rid itself of the idea of the prince who appears in the guise of the beggar." This supernaturalist frame Robinson portrays *is* the culprit and is itself the product of a dualism couched in terms of "substance" and "nature" in the creeds.

7. See Marcus J. Borg, *Jesus: A New Vision* (San Francisco: Harper & Row, 1987); Thomas Sheehan, *The First Coming: How the Kingdom of God Became Christianity* (New York: Random House, 1986).

8. Shunryu Suzuki, *Zen Mind, Beginner's Mind*, ed. T. Dixon (New York: Weatherhill, 1973), 21.

9. The book by Adolf von Harnack was given the English title *What Is Christianity?* (1901; reprint, Philadelphia: Fortress Press, 1986).

10. John Dillenberger and Claude Welch, *Protestant Christianity Interpreted Through Its Development* (New York: Charles Scribner's Sons, 1958), 208.

11. Alfred North Whitehead, *Science and the Modern Mind* (New York: Macmillan Co., 1927), 280ff.

12. Stumpf, *Socrates to Sartre*.

13. See Augustine, "On the Grace of Christ, and On Original Sin," *Nicene and Post-Nicene Fathers*, ed. P. Schaff (New York: Christian Literature Co., 1886), 5: 214–55.

14. Unpublished paper by John B. Cobb, Jr., "Post-Modern Social Policy." The Santa Barbara Conference was sponsored by the new Center for a Post-Modern World (Santa Barbara) and by the Center for Process Studies (Claremont). The conference was held in Santa Barbara, January 16–20, 1987.

15. Robert N. Bellah et al., *Habits of the Heart: Individualism and Commitment in America* (Berkeley: University of California Press, 1985), 143.

16. Ibid., 327.

17. John B. Cobb, Jr., *Process Theology as Political Theology* (Philadelphia: Westminster Press, 1982), 125–33. Cobb concludes: "Concern for the least and most powerless of our fellow creatures may at times save us from suicidal action! But ecological theology will insist that our concern for these creatures must not be motivated only by our desire for human welfare. It is this important element which a Kantian theology does not include." The last two sentences should arrest our attention, for they underscore and bring to light the failings of the anthropocentrism in Kant and in the modern worldview generally.

18. I would direct the reader's attention especially to Riane Eisler, *The Chalice and the Blade* (San Francisco: Harper & Row, 1987). The book provides a most comprehensive historical perspective on the issue of patriarchalism. What is more, the treatment is designed to prepare ground for a change of worldview from *androcracy* (Eisler's technical term for patriarchalism) to *gylany* (Eisler's new term for a perspective that links both halves of humanity on an equal basis rather than on the old androcratic basis of rank). Eisler concludes the work with a discussion of concrete ways a change in perspective may be brought about. Two books are to follow that will explore in greater detail methods of constructive change. Of special interest for readers of this volume is Eisler's discussion of patriarchalism as it relates to the relationship between the population explosion (linked as it is to the subjugation of women) and the environ-

mental crisis (pages 198ff.). I know of no work that makes a more convincing case for such a relationship on historical grounds. Upon reading her treatment, one is tempted to entertain the view that the single and most crucial element in the modern mentality that makes for the environmental crisis is patriarchalism, because of its singular contribution to the overpowering of the biosphere by too many humans. Women worldwide, claiming their full rights and status, could and would cut down the world's population.

19. Dietrich Bonhoeffer, *Letters and Papers from Prison*, ed. E. Bethge (New York: Macmillan Co., 1953), 279ff.

20. Ibid., 327.

CHAPTER 2. POSSIBILITIES AND PERSPECTIVES
FOR A NEW WORLDVIEW

1. Raghavan Iyer, *The Moral and Political Thought of Mahatma Gandhi* (New York and Oxford: Oxford University Press, 1978), 232.

2. Such interdisciplinary exploration occurred at the Santa Barbara Conference held in Santa Barbara, Calif., January 16–20, 1987.

3. Paul Tillich, *Morality and Beyond* (New York: Harper & Row, 1963), 20.

4. Fox, *Original Blessing*, 55. See also Frederick S. Perls, *Gestalt Therapy Verbatim* (Moab, Utah: Real People Press, 1969), 5–71 passim.

5. The reader may consult works by Ian Barbour, Charles Birch, David Bohm, Ken Butigen, John B. Cobb, Jr., Fredrick Ferré, Matthew Fox, David Ray Griffin, Philip N. Joranson, Carolyn Merchant, Arthur Peacocke, Michael Polanyi, Ilya Prigogine, Benjamin A. Reist, Harold Schilling, Charlene Spretnak, and Brian Swimme as examples.

6. Reist, "New Theological Horizons," 5.

7. Fox, *Original Blessing*, 90.

8. Harold Schilling, *The New Consciousness in Science and Religion* (Philadelphia: Pilgrim Press, 1973), 246. For an introduction to process thought, see John B. Cobb, Jr., and David Ray Griffin, *Process Theology: An Introductory Exposition* (Philadelphia: Westminster Press, 1976).

9. Arthur Peacocke, *God and the New Biology* (San Francisco: Harper & Row, 1986), 99. Graphically, Peacocke goes on to depict such an image of reality: "I would denote an area representing nature and would place that entirely within another area representing God, which would have to extend to the edges of the blackboard and, indeed, point beyond it (to infinity). When I came to depict man, I would have to place him with his feet placed firmly in nature but with self-consciousness (perhaps represented by his brain?) protruding beyond the boundary of nature and into the area that attempts to 'depict' God, or at least refer to him" (p. 96).

10. Paul F. Knitter, *No Other Name? A Critical Survey of Christian Attitudes Toward the World Religions* (Maryknoll, N.Y.: Orbis Books, 1985), 8.

11. Benjamin A. Reist, "Dogmatics in Process," *Pacific Theological Review* 11 (Spring 1986): 6.

12. Schilling, *The New Consciousness;* see also Peacocke, *God and the New Biology,* chap. 6.

13. Ian Barbour, *Issues in Science and Religion* (New York: Harper & Row, 1966), 304–305.

14. See, for example, Gary Zokav, *The Dancing Wu Li Masters: An Overview of the New Physics* (New York: William Morrow & Co., 1979); and Fritjof Capra, *The Tao of Physics* (New York: Shambhala, 1975).

15. Peacocke, *God and the New Biology,* 102.

16. Ibid., 101.

17. Fox, *Original Blessing,* passim. I summarize only some of the essentials of the rich and complex treatment by Fox. The reader is urged to explore the entire volume for its comprehensive exposition of the creation-centered tradition.

18. Morten T. Kelsey, *After Life: The Other Side of Dying* (New York: Crossroad, 1985), 84–85.

19. See especially Joranson and Butigen, *Cry of the Environment.*

20. Schilling, *The New Consciousness,* 44. Schilling characterizes the Newtonian world as "closed, essentially completed and unchanging, basically substantive, simple and shallow, and fundamentally unmysterious—a rigidly programed machine." Schilling goes on to investigate the mystery that is in reality at all levels and includes an extensive treatment of the word *mystery* itself at several places in the work. One is also struck by his employment of the word *intuition* regarding his treatment of the new physics.

21. For what follows see Sallie McFague, *Metaphorical Theology: Models of God in Religious Language* (Philadelphia: Fortress Press, 1982), 37–42. See also Sallie McFague, *Models of God: Theology for an Ecological, Nuclear Age* (Philadelphia: Fortress Press, 1987). Here, McFague carries forward the theses advanced in her other volume and brings the discussion into the arena of the environmental crisis. It addresses brilliantly the issues and arguments I attempt to treat in this book.

22. McFague, *Metaphorical Theology,* 218 n. 29.

23. Reist, "Dogmatics in Process," 18.

24. McFague, *Metaphorical Theology,* 190.

25. Thomas Merton, *New Seeds of Contemplation* (New York: New Directions, 1961), 290–97.

26. Fox, *A Spirituality Named* Compassion, chap. 2.

27. Ibid., 18.

CHAPTER 3. A SPIRITUALITY TO TRANSCEND
MODERN LIMITATIONS

1. See, for example: Borg, *Jesus: A New Vision*, chaps. 2–4; Edward Schillebeeckx, *Jesus: An Experiment in Christology* (New York: Crossroad, 1981), 256–68; Matthew Fox, *The Coming of the Cosmic Christ* (San Francisco: Harper & Row, 1988), 67–73; and Donald Goergen, *The Mission and Ministry of Jesus* (Wilmington: Michael Glazier, 1986), 129–45. Borg's treatment is especially instructive in its delineation of the context of Jesus' spirituality within the spiritual tradition of early Judaism. See also my Appendix in this volume.

2. See Albert Schweitzer, *The Mysticism of Paul the Apostle* (New York: Macmillan Co., 1931).

3. E. Kadloubovsky and G.E.H. Palmer, trans., *Writings from the Philokalia on the Prayer of the Heart* (London: Faber & Faber, 1977). For an understanding of the way Orthodox mysticism was embedded in early Greek theology before the *Philokalia* was created, see Vladimir Lossky, *The Mystical Theology of the Early Eastern Church* (Tuckahoe, N.Y.: St. Vladimir's Seminary Press, 1976).

4. *The Interpreter's Dictionary of the Bible*, s.v. "Mind."

5. William Johnston, *The Inner Eye of Love* (San Francisco: Harper & Row, 1978), 16.

6. Harry A. Wolfson, *The Philosophy of the Church Fathers* (Cambridge: Harvard University Press, 1970), chaps. 10–13.

7. Fox, *A Spirituality Named* Compassion, chap. 2. See also John of the Cross, *Dark Night of the Soul*, trans. E. A. Peers (Garden City, N.Y.: Image Books, 1959), 164ff.

8. John of the Cross, *Dark Night of the Soul*, 89–91.

9. I. Progoff, trans., *The Cloud of Unknowing* (New York: Delta, 1959).

10. Frank Laubach and Brother Lawrence, *Practicing His Presence* (Goleta, Calif.: Christian Books, 1968), 47, 56, 89. A good example of this type would be the work of Madame Jeanne Guyon, *Experiencing the Depths of Jesus Christ* (Goleta, Calif.: Christian Books, 1975).

11. For what follows, see Fox, *Original Blessing*, Paths 1–4, passim.

12. Johnston, *The Inner Eye of Love*, 154–64.

13. Ibid.

CHAPTER 4. AN ETHIC TO TRANSCEND
MODERN LIMITATIONS

1. Paul Lehmann, *Ethics in a Christian Context* (New York: Harper & Row, 1963), 23–25.

2. Robert McAfee Brown, *Saying Yes and Saying No: On Rendering to God and Caesar* (Philadelphia: Westminster Press, 1986), chap. 1.

3. Consider the question, Who is my enemy? The "enemy" may be anyone or any creature we seek to press into the confines of our own mold and way of doing things. Others we expect to be like our best image of ourselves become enemies in the twinkling of an eye. (Often this is done by projecting upon others traits we find disagreeable in ourselves and which we wish to disown through the process of projection. Thus, we project these faults upon others and then demand that they be rid of them.) If this be so, then loving the enemy means allowing the other to be "other" and learning to appreciate them for who and what they are and may become. (It means also that we learn to accept and love those traits in ourselves that we have considered disagreeable heretofore. It means loving the enemy as we learn to love ourselves—bumps and all!) In such manner, one emulates the Creator who obviously delights in and loves the incredible diversity of creation and its creatures.

4. Reist, "Dogmatics in Process," 20.

5. Dietrich Bonhoeffer, *Act and Being*, trans. B. Noble (New York: Harper & Row, 1956).

6. Dietrich Bonhoeffer, *Gesammelte Schriften 1*, ed. Eberhard Bethge (Munich: Chr. Kaiser, 1958), 147.

7. Bonhoeffer, *Ethics*, 68–70.

8. Lehmann, *Ethics in a Christian Context*, chap. 3.

9. Bonhoeffer, *Ethics*, 69.

10. Ibid., 63–67.

11. Ibid., 363–72.

12. Ibid., 69.

13. For a summary of Gandhi's own writings, see, Gandhi, *All Men Are Brothers: Autobiographical Reflections*, ed. Krishna Kripalani (New York: Continuum, 1987). An excellent commentary on these writings that provides insight into Gandhi's relevance for current global problems is J. D. Sethi, *Gandhi Today*, 2d ed. (Sahibabad: Vikas; New York: Advent Books, 1979). Sethi's analysis is unique in demonstrating (1) the interrelationship between all of Gandhi's basic concepts and (2) how this interrelationship alters perspectives on political, economic, social, and religious policies.

14. For excellent reading that augments what is suggested here, see John Seymour and Herbert Girardet, *Blueprint for a Green Planet: Your Practical Guide to Restoring the World's Environment* (Englewood Cliffs. N.J.: Prentice-Hall, 1987).

15. See Adam Daniel Finnerty, "The Shakertown Pledge," *Epiphany: A Journal of Faith and Insight* 1 (Fall 1980): 68ff.

16. Bonhoeffer, *Letters and Papers from Prison*, 383.

CHAPTER 5. MEDITATIONS ON A NEW BEGINNING

1. Brown, *Saying Yes and Saying No*, chap. 1.

2. Ibid., 31.

3. Ibid., 28.

4. Dillenberger and Welch, *Protestant Christianity Interpreted Through Its Development*, 53–56.

5. See, for example: John B. Cobb, Jr., *Beyond Dialogue: Toward a Mutual Transformation of Christianity and Buddhism* (Philadelphia: Fortress Press, 1982); Knitter, *No Other Name?*; and Ninian Smart, *Beyond Ideology: Religion and the Future of Western Civilization* (San Francisco: Harper & Row, 1981).

6. Matthew Fox, *Breakthrough: Meister Eckhart's Creation Spirituality in New Translation* (Garden City, N.Y.: Image Books, 1980), 363–72.

7. Roger von Oech, *A Whack on the Side of the Head: How to Unlock Your Mind for Innovation* (New York: Warner Books, 1983), 55.

APPENDIX.

1. F. C. Happhold, *Mysticism: A Study and an Anthology* (New York: Penguin Books, 1984), 72, 94–100.

2. See ibid., 46ff. Merton, *New Seeds of Contemplation*, 282–89; Thomas Merton, *Contemplative Prayer* (Garden City, N.Y.: Image Books, 1969), 75ff. Thomas Merton, *Zen and the Birds of Appetite* (New York: New Directions, 1968), 71–78.

BIBLIOGRAPHY

Augustine. *The City of God*. Translated by M. Dods. New York: The Modern Library, 1950.

Augustine. "On the Grace of Christ, and On Original Sin." *Nicene and Post-Nicene Fathers*. Edited by P. Schaff. New York: Christian Literature Co., 1886.

Barbour, Ian. *Issues in Science and Religion*. New York: Harper & Row, 1966.

Bellah, Robert, Richard Madsen, William M. Sullivan, Ann Swidler, and Steven M. Tipton. *Habits of the Heart: Individualism and Commitment in America*. Berkeley: University of California Press, 1985.

Bonhoeffer, Dietrich. *Act and Being*. Translated by B. Noble. New York: Harper & Row, 1956.

———. *Ethics*. Edited by Eberhard Bethge. New York: Macmillan Co., 1955.

———. *Gesammelte Schriften 1*. Edited by E. Bethge. Munich: Chr. Kaiser, 1958.

———. *Letters and Papers from Prison*. Edited by Eberhard Bethge. New York: Macmillan Co., 1953.

Borg, Marcus J. *Jesus: A New Vision*. San Francisco: Harper & Row, 1987.

Brown, Robert McAfee. *Saying Yes and Saying No: On Rendering to God and Caesar*. Philadelphia: Westminster Press, 1986.

Capra, Fritjof. *The Tao of Physics*. New York: Shambhala Books, 1975.

Cobb, John B., Jr. *Beyond Dialogue: Toward a Mutual Transformation of Christianity and Buddhism*. Philadelphia: Fortress Press, 1982.

———. *Process Theology as Political Theology*. Philadelphia: Westminster Press, 1982.

Cobb, John B., Jr., and David Ray Griffin. *Process Theology: An Introductory Exposition*. Philadelphia: Westminster Press, 1976.

Dillenberger, John, and Claude Welch. *Protestant Christianity Interpreted Through Its Development*. New York: Charles Scribner's Sons, 1958.

Eisler, Riane. *The Chalice and the Blade*. San Francisco: Harper & Row, 1987.

Finnerty, Adam Daniel. "The Shakertown Pledge." *Epiphany: A Journal of Faith and Insight* 1 (Fall 1980): 68ff.

Fox, Matthew. *A Spirituality Named* Compassion *and the Healing of the Global Village: Humpty Dumpty and Us*. Minneapolis: Winston Press, 1979.

———. *Breakthrough: Meister Eckhart's Creation Spirituality in New Translation*. Garden City, N.Y.: Image Books, 1980.

———. *The Coming of the Cosmic Christ: The Healing of Mother Earth and the Birth of a Global Renaissance*. San Francisco: Harper & Row, 1988.

———. *Original Blessing: A Primer in Creation Spirituality*. Santa Fe: Bear & Co., 1983.

Frankfort, Henry, et al. *Before Philosophy: The Intellectual Adventure of Ancient Man*. Harmondsworth, Eng.: Penguin Books, 1951.

Gandhi, Mohandas. *All Men Are Brothers: Autobiographical Reflections*. New York: Advent Books, 1979.

Goergen, Donald. *The Mission and Ministry of Jesus*. Wilmington: Michael Glazier, 1986.

Gribbin, John. *The Hole in the Sky: Man's Threat to the Ozone Layer*. New York: Bantam Books, 1988.

Guyon, Madame Jeanne. *Experiencing the Depths of Jesus Christ*. Goleta, Calif.: Christian Books, 1975.

Happhold, F. C. *Mysticism: A Study and an Anthology*. New York: Penguin Books, 1984.

Hodgson, Peter C., and Robert H. King. *Christian Theology: An Introduction to Its Traditions and Tasks*. Philadelphia: Fortress Press, 1985.

Iyer, Raghavan. *The Moral and Political Thought of Mahatma Gandhi*. New York and Oxford: Oxford University Press, 1978.

John of the Cross. *Dark Night of the Soul*. Translated by E. A. Peers. Garden City, N.Y.: Image Books, 1959.

Johnston, William. *The Inner Eye of Love*. San Francisco: Harper & Row, 1978.

Joranson, Philip N., and Ken Butigen. *Cry of the Environment: Rebuilding the Christian Creation Tradition*. Santa Fe: Bear & Co., 1984.

Kadloubovsky, E. and G.E.H. Palmer, trans. *Writings from the Philokalia on the Prayer of the Heart*. London: Faber & Faber, 1977.

Kaku, Michio, and Jennifer Trainer. *Beyond Einstein: The Cosmic Quest for the Theory of the Universe*. New York: Bantam Books, 1987.

Kelsey, Morten T. *After Life: The Other Side of Dying*. New York: Crossroad, 1985.

Knitter, Paul F. *No Other Name? A Critical Survey of Christian Attitudes Toward the World Religions*. Maryknoll, N.Y.: Orbis Books, 1985.

Laubach, Frank, and Brother Lawrence. *Practicing His Presence*. Goleta, Calif.: Christian Books, 1968.

Lehmann, Paul. *Ethics in a Christian Context*. New York: Harper & Row, 1963.

Lossky, Vladimir. *The Mystical Theology of the Early Eastern Church*. Tuckahoe, N.Y.: St. Vladimir's Press, 1976.

McDonagh, Sean. *To Care for the Earth*. Santa Fe: Bear & Co., 1986.

McFague, Sallie. *Metaphorical Theology: Models of God in Religious Language*. Philadelphia: Fortress Press, 1982.

————. *Models of God: Theology for an Ecological Nuclear Age*. Philadelphia: Fortress Press, 1987.

Marcus, Joel. "Entering into the Kingly Power of God." *The Journal of Biblical Literature* 107, no. 4 (December 1988): 663–75.

Merton, Thomas. *Contemplative Prayer*. Garden City, N.Y.: Image Books, 1969.

————. *New Seeds of Contemplation*. New York: New Directions, 1961.

————. *Zen and the Birds of Appetite*. New York: New Directions, 1968.

Mumford, Lewis. *The Pentagon of Power: The Myth of the Machine*. New York: Harcourt Brace Jovanovich, 1970.

Peacocke, Arthur. *God and the New Biology*. San Francisco: Harper & Row, 1986.

Perls, Frederick S. *Gestalt Therapy Verbatim*. Moab, Utah: Real People Press, 1969.

Progoff, I., ed. *The Cloud of Unknowing*. New York: Delta, 1959.

Reist, Benjamin A. "Dogmatics in Process." *Pacific Theological Review* 19 (Spring 1986).

————. "New Theological Horizons in the Light of Post-Modern Science." *Pacific Theological Review* 18 (Spring 1985).

Robinson, John A. T. *Honest to God*. Philadelphia: Westminster Press, 1963.

Schillebeeckx, Edward. *Jesus: An Experiment in Christology*. New York: Crossroad, 1981.

Schilling, Harold. *The New Consciousness in Science and Religion*. Philadelphia: Pilgrim Press, 1973.

Schweitzer, Albert. *The Mysticism of Paul the Apostle*. New York: Macmillan Co., 1931.

Seymour, John, and Herbert Girardet. *Blueprint for a Green Planet: Your Practical Guide to Restoring the Environment*. Englewood Cliffs, N.J.: Prentice-Hall, 1987.

Sheehan, Thomas. *The First Coming: How the Kingdom of God Became Christianity*. New York: Random House, 1986.

Smart, Ninian. *Beyond Ideology: Religion and the Future of Western Civilization*. San Francisco: Harper & Row, 1981.

————. *Worldviews: Crosscultural Explorations of Human Beliefs*. New York: Charles Scribner's Sons, 1983.

Stumpf, Samuel E. *Socrates to Sarte*. New York: McGraw-Hill, 1982.

Suzuki, Shunryu. *Zen Mind, Beginner's Mind.* Edited by T. Dixon. New York: Weatherhill, 1973.

Teilhard de Chardin, Pierre. *Prayer of the Universe.* New York: Harper & Row, 1965.

Tillich, Paul. *Morality and Beyond.* New York: Harper & Row, 1963.

von Harnack, Adolf. *What Is Christianity?* New York: Putnam, 1901. Reprint. Philadelphia: Fortress Press, 1986.

von Oech, Roger. *A Whack on the Side of the Head: How to Unlock the Mind for Innovation.* New York: Warner Books, 1983.

Whitehead, Alfred North. *Science and the Modern Mind.* New York: Macmillan Co., 1927.

Wolfson, Harry A. *The Philosophy of the Church Fathers.* Cambridge: Harvard University Press, 1970.

Zokav, Gary. *The Dancing Wu Li Masters: An Overview of the New Physics.* New York: William Morrow & Co., 1979.

INDEX